Advanced
Coarse Fishing

Advanced
Coarse Fishing

Graham Marsden

Second Edition
with a Foreword by
Peter Stone

A & C Black · London

A & C Black (Publishers) Limited
35 Bedford Row, London WC1R 4JH

Second edition 1987
First published 1980
Reprinted 1983

ISBN 0 7136 5593 3

Marsden, Graham
　　Advanced coarse fishing.—2nd ed.
　　1. Fishing
　　I. Title
　　799.1'2　　　　　SH439

　　ISBN 0–7136–5593–3

Printed and bound in Great Britain at
The Camelot Press Ltd, Southampton

Contents

FOREWORD

Graham Marsden is one of our most successful and respected anglers. I first 'noticed' Graham when I read his writings on big bream in his beloved Cheshire meres. His writings concerning outsize bream tallied with mine and I regard the bream chapter in this book as one of the most informative I have read.

Like many of today's successful specimen hunters, Graham ignores much of the advice and theories churned out by some older writers. He does not, for instance, regard patience as a virtue—quite the reverse in fact; 'many of today's successful anglers,' he says, 'are impatient men'. The shape of the bream, he says, was not as is generally believed designed for it to manoeuvre through bankside rushes, etc., but so it can shoal tightly—as bream do. 'I feel certain,' Graham says, 'the purpose of the slimness stems from the natural instinct to shoal in a compact body . . . it means a shoal of bream can pack tightly together and become a much smaller target . . . an almost unbroken "fence" of lateral lines, a natural radar system.'

This is not simply a 'how to catch them' book, it discusses fish behaviour too, and deep knowledge of how one's intended quarry behaves is a most important factor. Many books, often excellent in their own right, all too often exclude this vital information. Such knowledge however is gained only from experience and Graham Marsden has plenty of that.

Graham's sometimes often spectacular catches have resulted not from guesswork or luck but from close study of his chosen waters. Some of his observations—like outsize dace taking up position at the back of a shoal and a shoal of bream doing *exactly* what the leader up front does—are thought-provoking indeed. The book makes you think—as a good book should do.

But, he stresses, specimen hunting does not simply mean catching fish but enjoying oneself and the importance of good friends.

This book Graham says, is aimed at the budding specimen hunter. They (and not a few experienced 'hunters' too) will learn much from it.

Peter Stone

PREFACE TO THE SECOND EDITION

Since the first edition of this book there has been a tremendous amount of change in specimen hunting, not the least being that fishing for big fish is now called specialist angling. These days to refer to a specialist angler as a specimen hunter is like calling a radio a wireless. Even that most famous body of big fish men, the National Association of Specimen Groups (N.A.S.G.) has changed its name to the National Association of Specialist Anglers (N.A.S.A.)

Never mind, what's in a name, as they say, except the image?

Image, however, does play a very big part in today's big fish scene, but instead of the floppy hats and MK IV Carp rods of yesteryear, carbon rods and electronic gadgetry are the status symbols.

The longest forward strides have been trodden over carp fishing; particle baits, boilies, hair-rigs and bolt-rigs have appeared, which I have now written about in the carp chapter. However, I have still kept those few original paragraphs that describe a typical session using, what I term, classic methods. I would be the first one to admit, though, that modern methods are far more successful on most waters. But more enjoyable? Only you can decide.

I have added to the bream chapter, since I have learned about float fishing for big bream these past few years and feel I can point anyone in the right direction who fancies trying the method. Believe me, it can be very deadly and exceptionally rewarding.

Float fishing for big bream ties in very nicely with punt fishing, to which I have devoted a chapter, because punt fishing can be such a pleasure when set about properly (but such a pain when it is not). It is well worth knowing how to do it right.

I have also included the current record fish list according to N.A.S.A. When I first wrote this book the record list was in such a mess it was not worth printing, but now it is sorted out and the N.A.S.A. list has become established as the accurate and historically faithful one.

Apart from the aforementioned, all other chapters have been brought up to date, where necessary, with information about the latest tackle and techniques.

INTRODUCTION

I would like to think that this book will be especially useful to budding specimen hunters; to those anglers who have mastered the basic art and are looking forward to a stage beyond casual angling. After all, for those of us who are ambitious in most respects, there must come a time when 'chuck-and-chance-it' fishing begins to bore and become tedious; when we can no longer gain satisfaction from catching anything that comes along. The time must come when we want to take the luck out of angling and catch quality fish through careful thought and actions.

In almost all other sports the participants work to a plan. Can you imagine, for instance, a league football team playing opponents whose tactics they have not studied beforehand? It is much the same with fishing. To catch quality fish consistently you need to know as much about fish as possible; you need to study their basic habits and behaviour patterns. And then you must learn as much as you can about that particular species' habits in a particular water, which necessitates, of course, a study of the water too. You need to know the battlefield as well as the enemy.

But this rather grim metaphor I have used should not be taken to imply that fishing has to be a deadly serious business where good humour in the company of good friends has no place. Let us never forget that fishing is for fun, and no matter how seriously we treat the business of catching fish we should always go about it in good spirit.

I can honestly say that I get almost as much fun from the hunt as I do when I catch the fish. The close study of waters, the careful and methodical choice of swim, followed by the prolonged pre-baiting campaign I regard as much a part of my fishing as I do the actual presenting of my hook-bait.

There are some anglers who think that pre-baiting is completely unnecessary, and there are a few who regard any kind of groundbaiting, both prior to and during fishing, as a waste of time, money and effort. I am inclined to believe, though, that the anglers who profess to such notions are simply making excuses for the fact that they cannot be bothered to do it. If they doubt the value of pre-baiting they should bear in mind that it is possible to train fish to take food out of your hand if you hold a piece of food in the water for long enough and regularly enough.

It would be difficult, if not impossible, to train fish to such a high degree on waters which are fished regularly, and if it were possible it would only last as long as it took to hook the first fish. Not that we want to train fish to such an extent, but there is no doubt that we can teach fish to like certain foods, and where to find them. We can convince them that a food is safe, and then we can exploit the situation by presenting a hook-bait of the same food, in that spot, and know that if a fish comes along that has grown used to taking food there, it will not hesitate to sample our hook-bait. This is the whole essence of pre-baiting; to give fish a taste for a bait, which they become used to finding in a certain spot at a certain time. Anything that can do that cannot be unnecessary.

I do accept, however, that all fishing cannot be in a pre-baited swim. On some very popular waters you would probably find that someone else would reap the benefit of your time and expense. This is one of the reasons why, in some chapters in this book, you will find no reference to a pre-baiting campaign. Another reason is that there are a few instances where a pre-baiting effort would not be worth the time and trouble. On a river is a good example. If you know the river well enough and the swims where the particular species predominates, and you intend to use maggots as hook-bait—maggots which are thrown in by the gallon each week by other anglers fishing the water—then there is no point in pre-baiting with maggots. It is only worth pre-baiting in this instance if you intend trying to wean the fish in a particular swim onto a hook-bait to which they are not accustomed.

There has been a lot of debate over the years as to whether some anglers possess a sixth sense; a kind of extra sensory perception that consistently successful anglers use to full advantage when it comes to choosing a swim. It is supposed that these fortunate anglers can look at a piece of water, which can be devoid of all character, and say exactly where the fish can be found. I do not know if E.S.P. has anything to do with it, but I do know that I sometimes have a very strong urge to fish a certain swim that to all intents and purposes has no special feature that would normally attract me to it.

These hunches, which is another word for E.S.P., sometimes pay off; at other times they do not. At the least it could mean that my E.S.P. is a load of bunkum. At most it could mean that the times when I have been inexplicably drawn to a swim, and that swim has failed to produce, the fish at that time were not hungry. I doubt if any form of E.S.P. can tell you when fish are feeding or when they are not.

I do believe, however, that this theory of a sixth sense is not to be brushed aside lightly. While scientists and psychics continue to experiment and investigate, nobody has yet proved that E.S.P. is not a matter of coincidence or a figment of the imagination, nor has anyone conclusively proved that it is. Those who do believe in E.S.P., or a sixth sense, all agree that it is a phenomenon that has to be developed, and not something that you do or do not possess. I am open-minded enough to follow my instincts, or sixth sense, whenever the feeling comes over me. It pays off enough to make it worthwhile. And who knows, the more I pander to this sixth sense, if it does exist, the better I may develop it.

Having said that, I do not believe there is any substitute for cold logic based on the knowledge of a fish's habits and knowledge of waters. When it comes down to the man who fills his keepnet I would back the one who is prepared to study, prepare and pre-bait for his fish rather than the one who relies solely on a sixth sense, or mere guesswork.

It is customary these days to follow fashion, and this is no less true of anglers. If a well-known angler recommends a specific item of tackle for a certain style of fishing, a lot of anglers will blindly use that item even when it is totally wrong for the job in hand. The item was probably recommended in all sincerity and, indeed, could be a good thing to use in the right circumstances. But no one thing is right for all conditions.

Perhaps the best example is where rods are concerned. You may have a so-called angling personality who always fishes with a 7ft swing-tip rod that he uses for fishing the far bank of a 10ft-wide canal, but apart from that would do a better job on a

Christmas tree. But the number of anglers you see using this rod and trying to cast forty yards and more on a wind-swept reservoir is incredible. Then there is this latest vogue for stepped-up carp rods, which are fine if you are fishing with 15lb line for big carp in heavily-weeded water. Yet you see these big, heavy, whopper-stoppers being used with 6lb or 7lb line in open water.

Enjoyment should, however, be foremost in our minds. Without that we may as well pack in fishing and look for another sport. There is nothing worse than becoming too serious about any hobby, sport or pastime. It is fatal to lose sight of the fact that, basically, we go fishing to enable us to forget all about the hustle and bustle of everyday life and to lose ourselves in the pleasure of catching, or attempting to catch, fish.

Becoming too serious about fishing can lead to silliness. One angler I know through a friend who used to fish with him, changes his car and hat every few months so that he can remain unrecognised and nobody will follow him to his 'secret' water. When pre-baiting a swim he wades into the water some fifty yards or more from the swim and then scuttles along the margins. The idea of that, so he reckons, is to confuse spies who may track his footprints which he swears are known to everyone. He has a hell of an ego!

The escape I need each week from the complications of civilised life and work is one of the reasons I finished with match fishing some years ago. It became too much like big business, especially on the open match circuit where prizes are reckoned in hundreds of pounds. I was working to a clock five and sometimes six days a week, and it became too much like work on my one day of enjoyment to fish to a clock, whose alarm is a whistle that tells you when to cast in and when to pull out. It was very aggravating to have to hang around for the draw, which tells you where to fish and then, when the match had finished, to hang around again while the stewards weighed the catches and dished out the prize money.

Most matches ran for no longer than five hours, and while that was too long for a match I found it too short a time for fishing. I won a few prizes in the three seasons I fished contests, but I realised that if I wanted to become a first-class matchman I would have to dedicate myself to it and forget all about pleasure angling. It became obvious that whenever I went fishing, even when I was not taking part in a match, I would have to practice and fish match-fishing tactics. That I was not prepared to do.

So I turned to specimen hunting, something I could dedicate myself to without having to fish at set times on specified venues. I could, within reason, fish for what I wanted, where I wanted, and for as long as I liked. Let's face it, the real difference between a matchman and a big fish man is that the matchman enjoys the competition more than the fishing. With a big fish man it is exactly the opposite. There is sufficient competition from the big fish themselves.

A favourite saying of non-anglers is, 'You must have some patience to sit there all day fishing.' If that were true about fishing in general, then specimen hunting requires the patience of Job. It is not true though, at least as far as successful angling is concerned. The only patient anglers are those who fish regularly and catch nothing. You do need patience for that.

You will find that the most successful anglers are very impatient indeed, which is one reason why they are successful. They are not prepared to sit there all day fishing with a favourite bait or method, hoping the fish will decide to fit in with their ideas. A successful angler adjusts his baits and methods to fit in with the fish's ideas. He will change swims and tactics continuously until he discovers where the fish are and the kind of bait presentation needed to catch them.

But this does not mean that the successful angler has to go fishing looking as miserable as an undertaker in a maternity ward. Big fish can be angled for with a smile, if not a belly laugh, though jumping for joy on the lake-side or river bank is best delayed until the fishing is over.

I have put a lot of emphasis on the study of fish behaviour and getting to know the waters where you expect to catch them. After all, no amount of sophisticated tackle and techniques will catch fish if they are applied wrongly. Moreover, you can only apply them correctly if you know how to choose a productive swim.

Avoid falling into the trap of judging your results by the standards other anglers are setting on other waters. You will soon learn what the average size of fish is on a certain water, and if you consistently catch fish from there above that average then you can take pride in the fact.

By that I do not mean that if you are catching 8oz roach from a water where the average is 3oz, you are doing as well as the angler who is catching 2-pounders from a lake where they average 1½lb. I mean that you should not judge the merit of your 8oz roach by the 2lb roach from another water.

I hope you enjoy reading my book, and I hope, too, that it will help you to catch more and bigger fish whilst still retaining your sense of humour and a sense of values.

Part One: The tackle and the techniques

The Scientific Angler

In 1953 the late Richard Walker wrote a book called *Stillwater Angling* (David and Charles). It was the first book of its kind to link scientific data (if that is not too grand a term) with fishing. It dealt quite profoundly with the effect of wind on water, water temperature, temperature layers, and the seasonal changes.

Walker did not discover this scientific evidence, but he did relate what he knew happened in waters to the effect this vould have on fish. At a certain temperature he knew which species he would have more chance of catching. He knew where in a water there would be the most dissolved oxygen, and he knew, or made it his business to find out with a thermometer, where the warmest water could be found.

Over the years since *Stillwater Angling* was published there have been many criticisms about this scientific approach to angling. The popular comment is that science takes the fun out of fishing, and loses sight of the fact that fishing is a simple pastime. Perhaps the critics are those anglers that lend credence to the old adage of angling being 'A worm at one end and a fool at t'other.' If this attitude was fostered we would still be catching fish with bone hooks or crude harpoons.

Whether you approach fishing from a tactical, scientific angle, or with a simplistic, instinctual attitude, has nothing whatever to do with how much fun you get from your fishing. I go fishing for fun, and the thoughtful, calculated approach I adopt helps me to catch fish, and the more and bigger fish I catch the more fun I have. Of course, I do not always begin fishing by plumbing depths, taking temperatures, watching the

1

water for fish or signs of fish; especially on waters I have fished before. Sometimes I do not have the time, or even the inclination, but when I do I enjoy the collecting and sifting of infomation almost as much as I enjoy casting a line.

I really get great pleasure from launching an assault on a water I have never fished before. The weeks of planning, preparation and pre-baiting are done with dedicated enthusiasm. Depths and bottom make-up are checked with sonar equipment or plummet; maps are drawn up with these bottom contours clearly marked and the compass points indicated. Weedbeds and any other features such as sunken trees, feeder and outlet streams, springs, mussel beds etc. are all noted for my friends and I to ponder over and talk about through the week. Weekends in the close season are spent collecting this information; hours are spent watching the water for signs of fish; swims are cut out or stages built; bait is laid regularly during the final two or three weeks of the close season.

We try to evaluate what effect prevailing winds will have on certain swims; if the bank the sun hits first in the morning will be best; if a certain deep water area would pay off when the temperature has fallen below the significant 39.2°F; if a tree-lined bank will be devoid of fish once the autumn leaves have fallen; if there is a corner of the lake we can rope off when the bottom breaks and algae blankets the surface; if some swims are better fished from a boat with float tackle rather than from the bank with leger; if the area close to the spawning grounds will be best in the first week or two of the season.

These are some of the questions we ask ourselves and consider carefully before we begin to fish. Not every question on every occasion of course, but the relevant questions which will minimise the element of chance.

I take great interest in fishery management, not to the extent where I am qualified to give advice on the subject, but enough to reasonably assess the rights and wrongs of some of the things we anglers do. I only wish that every angler would concern himself with fishery management, even if it is only a passing interest, especially angling club officials, for it is a fascinating subject in its own right, apart from the obvious advantages to be gained from learning how best to manage our fisheries.

There are three main causes of fishery deterioration: pollution, abstraction and mismanagement, but not necessarily in that order. The major symptom of mismanagement is over-stocking, for there are so many anglers—and angling administrators—who believe that fish should feed every Sunday. When they don't it rarely occurs to them that there could have been a population explosion of some natural food creature with which the fish have become preoccupied, nor do they ever stop to think that fish need time to digest food as well as time to eat it. Nor would they ever consider fish to be so impertinent as to digest food on Sundays!

Whenever such an angler endures a longer than usual period of not getting bites, he has only one answer: 'Bung some more fish in,' and he will say at his club meeting, 'I haven't had a bite for weeks. All the fish are dead.' The cry for more fish to be stocked into the water is then taken up by all the other like-minded anglers at the meeting, and these in turn are joined in their exhortations by anglers who are only there for the beer, or those who care very little, but always go along with the majority. As a result, thousands of fish are planted in the unfortunate fishery. After a few seasons, only small fish are caught, much smaller than the average size of fish that used to be caught before the stocking took place, and everyone wonders why. When this comes about, those same anglers are the first to say, 'Bung some more fish in. Big 'uns this time.'

All farmers know that a field can provide for only a certain number of cows. Exceed that number and the cows will lose weight or suffer in other ways. Similarly, any fishery can only support healthily a certain poundage of fish per acre, be that poundage a hundred small fish or several big ones.

Whether you know anything about fishery management or not, the next time you go to a club meeting and someone wants to spend money on more fish for a water, do your best to make sure they take expert advice first. A few pounds spent wisely on ensuring that the right action is taken can be a sound investment for the future.

I like to read books about fishery management, fish biology, aquatic plants and animals; anything in fact that will give me a deeper insight into how fish think and behave, and therefore

3

help me to think like a fish and calculate the best ways of catching them in all kinds of situations.

I do not think of myself as a scientific angler, but rather an enthusiast who likes to leave as little as possible to chance. But it was T. H. Huxley (1825-1895) who said, 'Science is nothing but trained and organised common sense.' If that is true, then I *am* a scientific angler.

Tackle

In each chapter dealing with a species you will find I have recommended various types, sizes and strengths of rods, reels, lines, hooks and all other sundry items. Here, I am going to discuss tackle in more depth in the hope that it will help you to choose the best.

Whatever I have recommended, you should always bear in mind that to a great degree tackle is a personal affair. Guidelines can be laid out, but your own taste will decide what you will use, and this is especially true where rods are concerned, e.g. when long-range legering for all species other than carp and pike I favour a rod between 11ft and 11ft 6in. in length, a test-curve of a little over 1lb, with a fast-taper action. Such a rod casts long and accurately; picks up a long line without maniacal exertion, and remains soft enough in the tip to retain the necessary shock-absorber effect.

Not many years ago I would have considered this rod as too stiff, robbing me of the enjoyment of feeling and seeing a good fish put a decent bend into it. At that time I used an 11ft rod with a test-curve of ¾lb and an all-through, very supple action. I argued continually with another angler who swore by 11ft, 1½lb test-curve rods with a poker-like action. He referred to my rods as stepped-up fly rods, and his I called tent poles. We both had a point but neither would concede to the other. My argument was that he might as well use pit-props for his fishing, for he couldn't possibly gain any enjoyment from playing fish, or handling such a rod with no more than a 4lb line. He replied that it didn't matter a damn about that as long as he got the fish on the bank.

We lost touch for a couple of years and then we met at the Coventry Specimen Group Stag Night and found that each of us had conceded to an extent and were now using almost identical rods. I was using stiffer rods and he was using softer ones. The point of the story is that when I was using softer rods and he favoured stiffer ones we both caught, relatively speaking, no fewer fish than we do today. We are simply happier and more confident with our present choice of rod.

If you prefer a rod different to the one I have recommended; one which you use successfully and are happy and confident with, then stay with it until you feel like a change yourself. My recommendations are no more than guide-lines based on my own judgment and personal preference.

Cheap reels are not worth a second thought. You will have nothing but trouble with tangled and damaged lines, broken parts, and will never be able to cast and retrieve line with any efficiency. The expensive reels are not expensive in the long term, but each model has its points of merit. Some have more efficient clutches, some have better bale-arm mechanisms; better finishes or smoother gears. Some have bale-arm rollers and skirted spools. Some have wide spools which make for longer casting. Consider all the pros and cons and choose accordingly. But remember that the best reels, as in most things, are not cheap.

More than a decade ago you could have chosen the best nylon line from those manufactured as easily as sifting maggots from casters, there were so few good ones and so many bad ones. Today, there are more good lines than bad, and the choice amounts to little more than personal preference. The most important point to look for in a line—apart from the obvious one of reliability throughout its length—is suppleness. The more supple a line the more natural a bait will behave in the water. Other considerations are the least diameter for a given breaking strain; anti-kink properties; elasticity and colour. Most waters have dark bottoms, and a brown or tan line is most suitable. Elasticity is important: I do not always prefer a line which stretches the least. For short-line fishing I like to have a line with some stretch; it complements the shock-absorber effect of the rod. For long-range fishing you can do without the

6

elasticity, for picking up a long length of line and planting a hook is difficult enough without any 'give'. You should bear in mind, too, that the lines with the least stretch are less supple than lines with a lot of stretch. The answer here is to use the 'stiff' line on the reel, and a hook length of supple line. Also, some lines sink faster than others, so choose one type for legering and another for float fishing.

It has always been a source of amazement to me that anglers who are prepared to pay upwards of £100 for a rod and reel moan plaintively about the price of perhaps the most important item of tackle: the hook. Always inspect each hook closely before you use it; test it for breaking or bending; reduce or remove the barb where necessary, and work on it with a fine oil stone until it is as sharp as you can get it—this should not actually be necessary with the new chemically sharpened hooks.

Now that we have lead-free split-shot, which is more expensive than lead shot, more care goes into its manufacture and there should be few problems.

Floats should be inspected for good finish, secure rings and concentric shape. Recommended shot capacity is usually wrong; a consequence of mass production.

Use a large landing net, somewhat larger than the size of fish you hope to catch. How dreadful it would be if you hooked a big fish only to lose it through poking around with an inadequate net. Micro-mesh nets are best, both for the welfare of the fish and your own good temper, for wide-mesh nets have a nasty habit of ensnaring leger weights and shot.

Keepnets too, should be large, not necessarily in length but in width. Much of the damage caused by keepnets is due to most of them being too narrow, so that as the fish lashes its tail back and forth the mesh brushes the protective mucous off and gradually wears the fin away. A wide net helps to prevent this happening and also allows the fish to turn round if they want to. Better still, put them straight back, or, if you wish to retain the fish for a photo, use a keepsack.

A good tackle box is essential. Look for one that allows good organisation of all your bits and pieces, and gives easy access to them. It makes life a lot simpler.

7

Baskets for carrying your tackle box, reels, bait, flasks, sandwiches, etc., and for sitting on, are, I suppose, fine if you fish for only two or three hours at a stretch. Much more and you are well on your way to back-ache and a good candidate for lumbago, not to mention being downright uncomfortable, and your fishing will suffer as a consequence. Most pleasure anglers, especially regular night-anglers, use a rucksack to carry their gear and a bed-chair to sit or even lie on. For shorter sessions or for a wandering style on rivers, a combination chair/rucksack, fold-up stool or chair, are better.

There are two types of rod hold-all. The most common is the one with a large, single pocket for the rods and two or three smaller pockets for umbrella, rod-rests and bank-sticks. The other type is the roll-all, which opens out to allow you to slot the rods and other items into small pockets stitched along the bottom with tape ties to hold them in place. As the name suggests, you simply roll it up and strap it round. The roll-all is kinder to rods, especially the rings, but if you are absent-minded like me, they can tax your patience. I have an annoying habit of packing and then finding something I have overlooked, usually a rod-rest or bank-stick, which means having to undo three straps and unrolling the roll-all. It may not sound much, but if it is raining and you are wet and tired, it becomes a big job. With the hold-all you simply drop the item into the appropriate pocket and are away without delay. Choose one that incorporates plastic tubes to protect your rods.

Disgorgers are a minor but very important piece of tackle. For deeply hooked fish, the tubular, slotted type are best. For larger hooks, a good pair of curved surgical forceps cannot be bettered. You will also find them useful for other jobs that need a small locking clamp.

There are so many bite indicators for use when legering you would think there was something extremely complicated to the simple action of a fish pulling on the line. There are some really weird contraptions which have more levers, joints, and other paraphernalia than a Swiss watch. I have tried most of them, apart from the downright ridiculous ones, mainly from curiosity, but still find that a simple clip-on bobbin, or a good butt indicator, is best. If you fish either of these in conjunction

8

with an Optonic bite alarm, it makes for efficient, relaxing fishing. A clip-on bobbin with a Betalight is used at night, with the Optonic of course. For carp fishing at extreme long range, I use the needle-type, monkey-climb indicators, again with an Optonic.

I occasionally use a quiver-tip on stillwaters, but it is an indicator I find most valuable on rivers, except at those times when the fish are being very finicky, when I will touch-leger. (See chapter 'Touch Legering', page 12.)

There will come a time when you will want to fish with two rods, which means you will have to buy another rod and reel. Do not make the mistake of buying makes or models of tackle other than the ones you already have. I know that buying additional tackle gives you the opportunity to try something different, but it is not a good idea.

When you have used a certain rod for any length of time you become accustomed to its 'feel'. Where once you were making a conscious effort to cast long and accurately and were aware of the amount of punch you needed to put into the strike, you will find that with experience you begin to do these things quite naturally. If you buy a different second rod you will have to learn this all over again, but more important, when you are fishing with both rods you will never work with them instinctively. Each time you pick one up you will be checking which rod it is and adjusting your actions to suit that particular rod. Sometimes you have to strike very quickly, such as when fish are finicky and you have to respond to twitch bites. In this case you have no time to check which rod you are striking with and it could lose you fish if you strike too hard with the stiffer rod and break off, or too gently with the softer rod and fail to sink the hook.

It is not quite so important to duplicate the reel, but it is still wise, if only for the fact that your spare spools are interchangeable on both reels.

Any angler who specialises in big fish always weighs his fish. There is never any respect for an angler who says he 'estimated' the fish at such and such a weight, for his catches will always be regarded with suspicion, to say the least. Anyhow, it is only natural that an angler specialising in better quality fish should want to know *exactly* what they weigh.

For this you need a good spring balance, and most anglers, myself included, use a dial scale, which weighs up to about 30lb in 1oz divisions. You can get a metric version if you wish, but despite the conversion of practically everything to metric, metric scales in fishing are as rare as rocking horse droppings. Spring balances that weigh in excess of 30lb are available for those anglers who expect, or at least hope, to catch carp and pike heavier than 30lb.

Along with a spring balance you also need a weighing sling. These are specially designed to cradle the fish securely in a comfortable position without wiping away a great deal of their protective mucous. They are inexpensive and well worth buying to ensure fishes' welfare.

I have covered all the major items of tackle that warrant discussion, but before this chapter is concluded I think that a comparison of end tackles is worth looking at.

For most of my stillwater legering, except for carp, I favour a fixed paternoster rig. I prefer a paternoster for several reasons, some of which are fairly obvious, such as long and accurate casting and the simple way it copes with soft mud and weed. I also prefer it because I believe it is more sensitive than a link-leger and gives me a better chance of hooking fish.

There is a mistaken impression amongst many anglers that when a fish bites on a link-leger it pulls the line through the swivel. This is only true when the fish has taken up all the slack of the link and has met considerable resistance from the lead. In many instances, when a light lead is being used the fish will begin to move the lead before the line starts to run. With a paternoster, the fish will move the line to the indicator before it feels the lead.

Whenever I have argued this point with other anglers they inevitably say that all you need to do is use a long link and a short hook-length when link-legering to obtain the same effect. What they are saying, in effect, is change from a link-leger to a running paternoster, for whenever the lead is leading the hook it *is* a paternoster. Match anglers favour a 'paternoster' (as they call it) with a long hook length and a short bomb length, which, really, is a fixed link-leger.

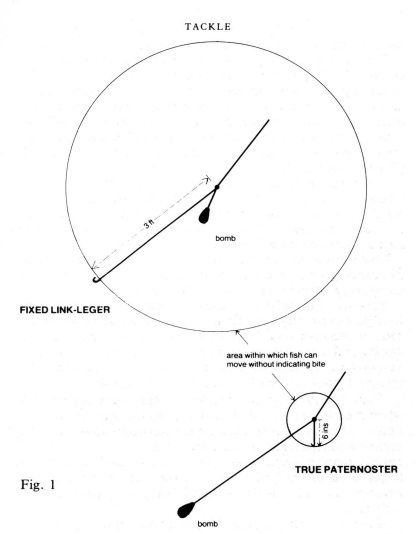

Fig. 1

The paternoster I use is the genuine article, which entails a long bomb length and a short hook length. The match angler's fixed link-leger is less sensitive than a fixed paternoster as can be appreciated by studying Fig. 1. The long hook length, however, of the fixed link-leger, is the best one to use when fish are feeding 'on the drop'. (For details of the hair-rig and bolt-rig, see the chapter on Carp.)

Touch Legering

There are a great many misconceptions about touch legering, stemming mainly from the conclusions drawn by anglers who have never tried it, or who have tried it and failed to catch fish. Touch legering means, quite simply, that you hold the line and feel for bites instead of relying on some kind of visual indication.

Touch legering, like so many things worth doing, needs to be practised before you can expect to be proficient. I would not expect an angler to hit, or even see, every bite he has on a swing-tip the first time he uses one. Nor do I expect an angler to recognise every bite he feels the first time he tries touch legering. After a while you learn to recognise the difference between a leaf brushing against the line and a fish gently mouthing the bait, just the same as you are now able to tell the difference between bites and false bites when your usual indicator moves.

Once you have mastered touch legering you will always be grateful you took the time and trouble to learn, for you will meet situations where, because of this experience, you are the only person catching fish on certain days when the fish are not biting boldly enough to give a good visual indication.

I have heard a lot of silly arguments from anglers who cannot be bothered to learn touch legering. Their favourites are: 'It's useless in winter when your fingers are numb with cold.' 'I couldn't sit there all day holding the rod and feeling for only one or two bites, which is all you get on the water I fish,' and, 'I'd like to see anyone catch fish from my local cut when touch legering.'

Touch legering.

These arguments stem from ignorance and the mistaken impression that touch legering is advocated as the answer to all legering situations. It is not, any more than the swing- and quiver-tip are not the answer to everything. One thing is certain though; if I had to choose between touch legering and swing-tipping for all my fishing, the swing-tip would be second choice. Yet some anglers think that the swing-tip is God's answer to all indicators. The times when I see a swing-tip being used on a fast river, with the tip fully straightened, and therefore its usefulness cancelled out, is unbelievable.

There are three ways of touch legering. One is to hook a loop of line pulled from between butt-ring and reel over your finger. The second is to lightly grip this loop of line between finger and thumb, and the third is to hook the line over the index finger of the hand holding the rod (See Fig. 2). I have tried them all and find that the first method suits me best. You may favour a different way, but try them all and see. Actually, my middle

13

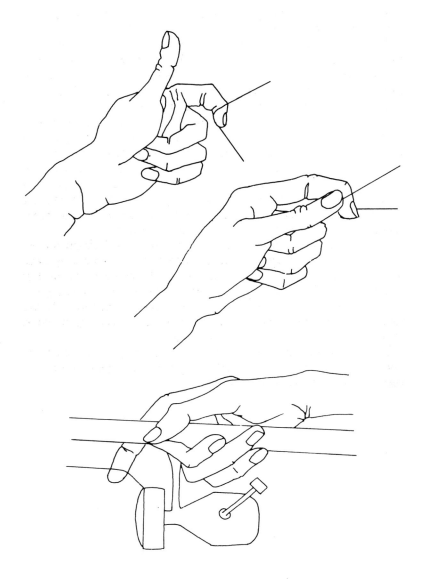

Fig. 2

14

finger is more sensitive than my index finger, so this is something else you must discover for yourself.

Ideally, when touch legering, the rod should be pointing directly at the bait, so that the line does not have to travel over any angles. If this is not possible, as is so often the case when fishing a near bank swim, don't worry; you will still feel the bites at the same time you see the rod-tip move.

Touch legering is not simply just a good idea because it is a sensitive way of detecting bites; it can also be extremely useful when the fish need slack line after mouthing the bait. If you are holding a loop of line from the reel, and you feel a bite, you can feed this loop to the fish until you know it is time to strike. No mechanical indicator can tell you the right time to strike, at least in this situation, but your sense of touch can, once you have enough experience to know what you are feeling for.

When you decide to practice, do not choose a difficult water, or difficult fish, where you are likely to have to wait a long time for a bite. Choose an easy water, where the fish are not too big and therefore fairly easy; a place where you know you can get a lot of bites. You can practice on the bigger fish with all the variations of bites that go with them, after you gain some experience of the basics with smaller fish.

Finally, make sure the fish are feeding first by catching one or two with your usual indicator. It is pointless to practice touch legering if the fish are not biting.

Night Fishing

I am often asked why I go night fishing, and it is too easy to say it
is because my chances of catching big fish are greatly increased
at night. I do not think they are; not in the night itself anyhow.

It would be more accurate to say I have caught more big fish
in daylight than in darkness, but that a lot of my daylight fish
came as a result of fishing all night. It sounds paradoxical I
know, but I will explain.

When I go for a night session I make sure to arrive well before
darkness, usually around 7.30 p.m. or 8 p.m. in summer, when
dusk does not fall until 10 p.m. or so. By the time I have layed
my groundbait, tackled up, and generally settled in it will be
turned 9 p.m.

There are two known periods when fish tend to feed more
than any other time in the summer months. These are dusk to
around 1.30 a.m., and from first glimmer of light to an hour or
so after sun-up. By arriving early in the evening I can fish both
periods, and it would be time-consuming and much more tiring
to get out of bed in the middle of the night to arrive at the water
before first light and to stay until 1.30 the following morning.
Night fishing entails about twelve hours at the water to fish the
best times. Daytime fishing entails at least twenty hours,
probably more, to fish the best times. I could not do this and fish
efficiently. Most anglers who do not night fish settle for either
evening or morning, rarely both.

Newcomers to night fishing are always surprised to find how
cold it is at night, especially those few hours before and after
dawn. It is thoroughly bone-chilling on nights of the full moon

when there are cloudless skies. A touch of ground frost is not uncommon, irrespective of how blazing hot it has been during the day.

Always take at least one heavy, woollen pullover with you, and a warm waterproof jacket. It needs to be waterproof, for hot days bring mist-shrouded nights, heavy with dew. You can get wetter than if you had been in a winter shower. Waterproof trousers and a pair of good boots or waders are essential too. Myself, I prefer a one-piece suit. Mine is quilted, waterproof and very warm. A one-piece suit also has the added advantage of keeping your pullovers pulled down over your back, leaving no gaps for the cold air to creep in. I would not be without it now.

Electric bite alarms are useful for night fishing, and many night anglers I know would not fish without them, and no matter what they tell you to the contrary they are mainly used to wake you up when you have a bite! They do have other uses of course, such as giving you an early, audible warning of a bite you have not yet seen, and allow you to attend to other things like pouring a cup of coffee and watering the horse, without the risk of missing a bite.

If you must use a light to illuminate your indicators then make it a dull, red one. A bicycle lamp with the glass painted red is ideal. The more you can avoid using lights, especially bright ones, the better chance your eyes have of adjusting to the darkness, making every move you make easier and more pleasing.

I would strongly recommend, where club rules allow, that you take a small stove and tea-brewing equipment. A fresh brew of tea, especially in the early morning, makes one hell of a difference to your well-being. The better you feel, the better you will fish and the more you will enjoy it. But by all means take a flask of tea or coffee to drink during the first few hours, but flasked drinks always taste stale after ten or twelve hours.

Arriving early for a night session is a good idea for several reasons, not least those I have mentioned about having plenty of time to tackle up in daylight, bait the swim, and settle in comfortably. I always like to take my time when I go fishing, to tackle up and bait the swim in a relaxed, easy-going manner. If I rush it unsettles me for the whole session, and I invariably feel

17

Pre-baiting the mere the evening before fishing.

as though I have not done something right. Very often I sit in my chair for ten minutes or so as soon as I arrive at the water, just relaxing and taking in everything around me, appreciating my surroundings and thinking about what I am going to do. Thereafter it is surprising how much better and easier I do things, with a greater feeling of being in control of the situation.

After tackling up and laying your baitboxes, landing net etc, around you, and sinking your keepnet in deep-enough water, you should still have a reasonable amount of daylight left to assess your surroundings. This is very important in a swim you have never fished before; on a known swim it reaffirms your acquaintance.

You should check the rushes, bushes and tree branches, if

18

any, behind you and establish just where you have to stand to cast without snagging when you lay the rod back. You should cast several times in daylight to get a feel of the power you need to put into the cast to reach the swim. But you should cast to the swim using a silhouette marker on the horizon, thus giving you practice for when you have to use the same silhouette for guidance in darkness.

I never go fishing without a watch. Noting the times when you get a bite or catch fish is especially useful for night fishing, for you soon learn which are the productive periods and which are the dead times. From this you can then judge when you can risk sleeping for an hour or two and so be much fresher for the more likely feeding times.

I am not too fond of fishing on my own at any time, and I really dislike it at night. It is not a question of being frightened of the dark (although it can be pretty spooky on an out-of-the-way water), it is because I enjoy good company and a long night becomes more enjoyable with someone there to chat with; to share the pleasure of catching big fish, or the lesser pleasure of blanking.

One of my best catches of big bream, five to 11lb 1oz and only one less than 9lb at 8lb 14oz, came when I was fishing alone. With a companion I am sure I could have doubled the catch. The fish were feeding ravenously, and several times when I was landing or unhooking fish the indicator on my other rod went sailing up.

You may think that instead of increasing my catch I would have had to share what I caught with a companion. I do not think so, for the fish were feeding too well, but I can honestly say I would not have minded sharing what I caught anyway. Enjoying my fishing, including the enjoyment I would have derived from seeing a friend catch, is more important to me than compiling a longer list of big fish than anyone else. The long lists of 'doubles' (usually carp) that some anglers publish each season do not impress me at all. It is not as though they are paid a bonus for this production-line fishing.

A companion on a night fishing session can be a great help too. Many times you will be glad of the extra pair of hands, such as when you need both your hands to play a big fish to the net that your mate can hold ready. Think, too, of the extra pleasure when you can do the same for him. You are not match fishing; you are there to help each other and share the pleasure of each other's fish. It has been said that it is unsporting to receive help from another angler when you catch a fish. Well, I do not fish for medals, I fish for pleasure, and while my mates like to net my fish as I like to net theirs, I care very little about petty-minded, selfish 'rules'.

An added bonus of fishing with a mate is that both of you will no doubt be fishing with an experimental bait or method on your second rod, so this means you can learn twice as much without having to fish with more than two rods yourself. Again, if you fish with a regular mate you can cut down on what you have to carry. You need only one landing net, one keepnet, one set of scales, etc. if you fish close to each other.

Night fishing can be enjoyable in its own right, even without the added attraction of fishing at the most likely times for fish to feed, but only if you go about it the right way.

Learn a lesson from a lad I know, who did just about everything wrong. He went to fish a water he knew nothing about, and arrived in darkness. He threw in a bucket of groundbait, a pint of maggots, and fished all night without a bite. When it broke daylight the next morning he found he had been fishing on a sandbar which shallowed up twenty yards out. His bait had been lying in three inches of water!

Punt Fishing

Fishing from a punt opens up a whole new world. You will find you have access to swims you once only dreamed about and it becomes possible for you to float fish in swims which can only be fished with leger tackle from the bank.

Before I discuss the technique of punt fishing, however, let me describe what kind of punt is ideal, and then you will know what to look for if you are about to buy one, or know what to plan if you are a good D.I.Y. man and intend building one.

My friend Eric Barnes built the punt we use and the basic design is hard to beat. The length and width will depend on how many will be using the punt at any one time, but always remember that they are not the easiest things to row, especially in rough water, so make a length of about 14ft your limit, with a width of about 4ft 6in. maximum.

It should, of course, be flat-bottomed, and should be carpeted. No, don't laugh; the carpet deadens the noise and vibration caused when objects are dropped, and believe me, a noise emanating from a punt is well magnified through the water. A punt is like a floating drum.

The carpet will inevitably get wet, but so what, you will have waterproof boots on, won't you? And a wet carpet still does the job it was meant for, which also includes the fact that it provides a soft base on which to unhook fish, preventing to a great extent the removal of mucous and damage to scales and fins.

We have covered around the edge of the punt with pipe insulation, which again cuts down noise and helps to preserve rod varnish. It was a simple matter of slitting along the length of the tubed insulation and sliding it onto the edge. And at two strategic points along each side of the punt are metal tubes into which can be slid umbrella poles or banksticks. Along the edge of the carpet are half-inch laths; these prevent your chair from sliding off the edge, which is not only noisy but quite hazardous, too, if you should lose your balance.

If you do, or intend to do, a lot of punt fishing, I would suggest that an outboard motor is a wise investment. Rowing a flat-bottomed punt in rough water, against a strong wind, is nigh on impossible on your own, and a back-breaking task even for two.

Now, apart from the noise and pollution, a petrol-driven outboard is usually unnecessary for punt fishing, for we rarely use a punt to reach very distant areas. The answer is an electric outboard motor. It runs off a normal car battery and has ample power to drive the punt at a greater rate of knots than you are likely to need, unless you are going to troll for pike; and then you would be better using a boat rather than a punt.

The electric outboard I use is made by Shakespeare. It has five forward and five reverse speeds, is highly manoeuvrable, and weighs less than the battery that powers it. One charge of the battery lasts for hours, even at top speed, and, of course, it is silent and pollution-free.

Another wise investment is a life-jacket, for no matter how strong a swimmer you may be you cannot swim if you are well wrapped up against the cold. In any case, you can buy life-jackets now that look little different from normal fishing waistcoats, so what is the point of being without and risking your life?

Anchors for the punt need only be heavy weights. The hook type do not work in the soft silt of most coarse fish waters. We use big plastic toffee bottles filled with concrete, with an eye-bolt sunk into the top.

You need an anchor at each end of the punt, on a variable length of rope so that you can fish at any depth of swim on the water. But better still, if you decide you are going to fish the same one or two swims each time, is to set up permanent anchors.

These are simple to prepare. All you do is rig up a normal

22

anchor, i.e. heavy weight, and rope. At the other end of the rope tie on a plastic, tightly-capped bottle. The distance from bottle to anchor should be about 1ft deeper than the depth of water. Leave another yard or so of rope above the bottle. Drop the anchors overboard in the correct position and the bottles will float, holding the anchor rope on the surface and ready to tie to the punt every time you fish that swim. On shallow swims it is better to sink two rigid poles (scaffolding poles are ideal), for with any rope-anchored system there is always a certain amount of swinging, especially when there is a strong wind.

Another advantage of being able to tie the punt to stakes so that it remains still is that you can then leger fish, which is otherwise impossible to do correctly due to the punt swinging around and giving false bites. Impossible, that is, if you rest the rod on the gunwales of the punt. But there is another way, and that is to use very long, extending rod rests (I use telescopic landing net handles) so that you can position the rod to one end of the punt, but within reach. Or, you can have the rod rests one either side of the gunwales so that the rod lies across, but clear of, the punt.

When legering from a punt you don't want to be messing about with indicators that require two hands to set. Movement in a punt should always be kept to a minimum. The best type, therefore, are swingtips, quivertips, and butt-indicators, which are permanently fixed to the rod and line and require no setting other than turning the reel.

Finally, remember that fishing from a punt gives you a tremendous advantage. So, use it to the full and explore all those spots you could never reach from the bank.

Record Fish

Many people are of the opinion that record fish lists exist mainly to bolster the egos of the captors of these huge fish. This sort
of attitude does angling no good at all. Record fish lists exist
purely as historical records. They are necessary to register the
heaviest fish of each species ever caught on rod and line; when
they were caught; where they were caught (although usually
vaguely); and, finally, by whom.

Unlike most records of sporting achievements, to appear in a
record fish list is no measure of an individual's skill. The simple
truth is that most captors of record fish were never heard of
before their historical catch and have never been heard of since.
It is important, however, that we keep accurate records, though
it is not so important we make rigid rules that can preclude the
recording of a well-authenticated fish simply because a rule was
not strictly adhered to.

It is for this reason we currently have the ludicrous situation
of two record fish lists, one run by the National Anglers Coun-
cil, which is a record of fish that were claimed in accordance
with a set of inflexible rules, and one that is run by the National
Association of Specialist Anglers, whose record fish appear according to individual merit, this merit being judged by highly
experienced specialist anglers who know a 'con' when they see
one and who would reject a claim if there were any doubt as to
its truth. N.A.S.A. members are more concerned than anyone
else that all record fish lists are genuine historical records.

The outcome is that in recent years the N.A.C. list has been
ignored by serious anglers who are aware of the N.A.S.A. list,

to the extent that in many instances the weights recorded for each species in the two lists are quite different. Perhaps the best example is Chris Yates' carp of 51 ½lb on the N.A.S.A. list and Dick Walker's carp of 44lb on the N.A.C. list. The late Dick Walker actually demanded that his fish be removed from the N.A.C. list, for he knew, as did everyone else, that his 44-pounder was not the largest carp ever caught on rod and line in Britain.

Here is the N.A.S.A. National Coarse Fish Record List, which is recognised as the official list by most anglers, particularly the specialist angler.

Species	Weight			Captor	Date	Location
	lb	oz	dr			
Barbel	14	6	0	A.D. Tyron	1934	Royalty, Hants, Avon.
Bleak		4	4	B. Derrington	1982	R. Monmow, Wye, Month.
Bream, Common	16	6	0	A. Bromley	1986	Staffordshire Mere.
Bream, Silver	Vacant (minimum claim 1lb)					
Carp	51	8	0	C. Yates	1980	Redmire Pool.
Carp, Crucian	5	10	8	G. Halls	1976	Lake near Kings Lynn, Norfolk.
Catfish (Wels)	43	8	0	R.J. Bray	1970	Wilstone Res, Tring, Herts.
Chub	8	4	0	G.F. Smith	1913	Royalty, Hants, Avon.
Dace	1	4	4	J.L. Gasson	1960	Little Ouse, Thetford, Norfolk.
Eel	11	2	0	S. Terry	1978	Kingfisher Lake, Ringwood, Hants.
Gudgeon		4	4	M.J. Brown	1977	Fish Pond, Ebbw Vale, Gwent.
Orfe, Golden	5	6	0	M. Foot	1978	Kingsley, Hants.
Perch	5	9	0	J. Shayler	1985	Private Water, Kent.
Pike*	42	2	0	D. Ames	1985	River Thurne, Norfolk.
Roach	4	1	0	R.G. Jones	1975	Gravel pit, Notts.
Rudd	4	8	0	Rev. E.C. Alston	1933	Thetford, Norfolk.
Ruffe		5	4	R.J. Jenkins	1980	West View Farm, Cumbria.
Tench	12	8	11	A. Wilson	1985	Wilstone Res, Tring, Herts.
Walleye	11	12	0	F.A. Adams	1934	The Delph, Welney, Norfolk.
Zander	17	12	0	D. Litton	1977	Great Ouse, Relief Channel, Norfolk.

*New pike record awaiting confirmation: 44lb 12oz, M. Linton, 1987, Ardleigh Reservoir.

Part Two: The fish

Barbel

One of my favourite species is the bream, not for his superior fighting power, for he does not test my tackle to any great degree, but because he tests my thinking power to the limit.

At the opposite end of the scale is the barbel, and while he does not require to be outwitted to the same extent as bream, he does make landing him extremely difficult. His sheer aggression on the end of a line makes him, too, one of my favourite species.

You have only to look at the shape and solidness of a barbel to see where he gets his speed and power. He could be described as an aquatic Concorde. The drooping snout and the torpedo-like body, coupled with big fins and muscles like Charles Atlas, make him one of the best, if not *the* best, fighting coarse fish.

The barbel takes his name from the four long whisker-like barbules that hang from his snout. These fleshy appendages are used to detect and taste food amongst the weed and debris on the bottom of a river. Though they are basically bottom feeders, there are times when they will feed at mid-water and sometimes at the surface. Such occasions are not the rule though, for their whole design suggests a fish that is more at home when his hollow belly is gripping the bottom and the surging current is pushing down on his drooping snout and coursing past his streamlined body.

The biggest authenticated barbel caught in Britain on rod and line weighed 16lb 10z, and was taken from the Hampshire Avon by a salmon angler. It was caught in the coarse fish closed season and did not qualify for record status. The official record is 14lb 6oz. Some well-respected names in fishing reckon they have seen barbel bigger than this, as much as 20lb in fact.

26

I reckon, however, that a barbel is a specimen when it weighs more than 7lb, though a 7lb barbel from the Severn is obviously a more rewarding catch than one of the same weight from the Hampshire Avon or Dorset Stour where the average weight is higher.

Barbel can be caught in huge numbers, a 100lb net not being especially unusual from a prolific barbel river like the middle reaches of the Severn. But the presence of a lot of barbel is not the only reason why large numbers can be caught at a sitting. These fish are especially prone to 'conditioning'; you can switch their minds onto a certain item of food and if you keep that food trickling through their swims over a long period they will continue feeding, with only short breaks, until that food runs out or some other disaster happens to move them. Even hooking and losing fish in the middle of a shoal does not put them off when they are feeding ravenously. Their minds are so preoccupied with feeding they ignore all but a monumental catastrophe. Yet it is as though some unseen power is switching them on and off. The usual pattern is that you take several fish one after the other, and then nothing for perhaps an hour, then several more fish in quick succession, and so on, until either you run out of bait or you have caught the whole shoal.

But you should not make the mistake of thinking it is always as easy as that. More often than not you have to work hard for a few fish. Even so, I have noticed that the feeding pattern still follows the usual course in that you catch barbel for a spell (maybe only one or two fish) then nothing for a spell, and so on. It very rarely happens that you take several fish in one period and then nothing for the remainder of the time you spend on the water.

You will have gathered from what I have said that barbel really are a true shoal fish, and it is true to say that, as is the case with all true shoal fish, they school together with fish of like size. This means that if you begin catching barbel in the 3lb to 4lb class you are unlikely to take any barbel very much bigger—or smaller—while that shoal remains in the swim. But this does not indicate that the particular swim where you are catching 3lb to 4lb barbel will only produce fish in that size range, for once that shoal moves out it is not unusual for another shoal to move in, be they bigger or smaller.

27

What you must beware of, however, is using all your bait on a massive shoal of small barbel. These fish in the 1lb to 2lb class can be a hundred or more strong in a shoal, and if you begin catching this size of barbel it is likely they will remain in the swim, feeding off and on, for as long as you have bait to keep them interested. As the size of barbel in a shoal becomes larger, so the number of fish in that shoal will be fewer. So if you begin catching barbel in the 4lb or larger bracket it is well worth sticking it out until they move on or you have caught most of them. When that happens there is a chance that the larger barbel will move in.

Once you have conditioned barbel to feed ravenously they are ridiculously easy to catch, assuming of course that you are using tackle which is adequate enough to handle these tremendously hard-fighting fish. The tackle should be compatible with the size of fish you hope to catch and the type of water you are trying to pull them from. Obviously, you will need much heavier tackle when fishing in snaggy water than you will in open water. Even so, barbel hooked in open water can tax tackle to the limit and it is foolhardy to take any chances with them.

Normally, and especially when the barbel are feeding with wild abandon, barbel bites on leger tackle are unmistakable, un-missable, and downright savage. A rod that is propped at 45° to the water, quivering slightly as the current pushes against the line, will suddenly slam over as though it has been struck with a sandbag. Woe betide anyone who is foolish enough to leave his rod unattended when barbel fishing. It is not unknown for barbel to pull a rod into the water with a speed and viciousness that has to be seen to be believed, even when the angler has only glanced away from his rod for a few seconds.

Rod-bending bites, although more common when barbel fishing than any other kind, are not the only sort of bite that these fish give. At the opposite end of the scale is a bite that is very difficult to detect if you are not conversant with the art of touch-legering (see pages 14-17). There is no pronounced tug of any kind, just a tremor coming up the line that feels as though someone is drawing a hacksaw blade across it. The strange thing is that these bites are not difficult to hit once you have detected them.

28

The rod-bending bites are merely the start of a run, and it is this first powerful run, which began as soon as the barbel picked up the baited hook and gained momentum within seconds, that is the crucial time for losing fish. It is almost impossible to stop this initial run without tearing the hook out of the fish's mouth, and yet you must not let the barbel have all his own way. If you do he will head straight for the nearest snag and you will be extremely fortunate to pull him out again.

In my experience the most effective way to resist his attempts to snag you is to heave at him with as much side-strain as your tackle strength will allow. A straight over-the-shoulder pull is ineffective, for the barbel is built to resist forces which act directly, head-on, against him. Your only chance is to pull at him from the side, which may steer him away from the refuge he seeks.

If you do manage it, the fight is by no means over. As the song says, it has only just begun. Time and time again he will charge for the snags which are in range, including some of which you may be unaware, or others you may think are out of range. Each time you should apply side-strain and try to steer him away from them. This is no time for delicacy and posing, it is time for strong-arm stuff which would bring looks of admiration from a shark angler and cause a tiddler snatcher to cringe in fear. Even when you think you have beaten him you should always be wary of a final fling, which invariably they can find the strength to muster. Your reflexes should always be in fine tune so that you can react appropriately to whatever action the barbel tries to take. Show him who is boss, or he will undoubtedly show you.

A very careful choice of rod should be made for a fish that fights as hard as barbel. Whilst it needs to be a powerful rod the emphasis should also be on the action. A rod which is too stiff is useless when it cannot react to a sudden, savage pull. One that is too supple will be equally useless when you need to apply swift, instantly effective side-strain.

It is wise to remember that the basic requirement of a rod, apart from the obvious ones of enabling you to cast and retrieve, is to act as a shock-absorber for the line. If the only consideration were strength then we need to look no further than a light pit-prop, for there is no freshwater fish swimming that could bend or break one of those.

If we had superhuman reactions then perhaps we could manage with a rigid pole, for we would then be fast enough to ease off when the fish made a sudden plunge. But we mere mortals need a rod that will give when this happens; a rod that will absorb the shock the instant a powerful fish pulls against the line. Since most barbel fishing is with the use of legering methods involving the rod tip as a bite indicator, some consideration should also be given to this.

A combination of these requirements can be found in a rod that is supple in its top half, but not too supple in the bottom half. The top section will then be suitable for bite indication and provide the shock-absorber effect; the bottom half will provide the power needed to turn a hard-fighting fish. A carbon-fibre rod, two piece, and a length of 11ft is my ideal.

Barbel inhabit all kinds of swims in a river, from the fastest run to the slackest pools. Big barbel though, have a distinct preference for swims that combine three factors: a fairly slack piece of water adjacent to a fast run, and especially where these two preside over a dense weedbed or some other kind of refuge such as a hole, steep ledge or sunken tree. The barbel will not be far away from the snag, and the closer you can fish to it with safety the better your chances are of catching these big fish.

There are times when barbel are so preoccupied with whatever business they have at hand, whether it be feeding, spawning, or just browsing, you can stand on the river's edge right over the top of them and watch them without them taking fright and scurrying off. If you can get so close to barbel, with or without them knowing it, you should take the opportunity to study how they use the available cover to sneak under; how they move like silent wraiths across the bottom, and how they rake over the gravel on the bottom with their barbules. It is interesting to note that when they do discover some titbit amongst the bottom debris, they very rarely charge off with it as they normally do when picking up our hookbaits. There is no doubt that their super-sensitive barbules detect our lines just as easily as they detect food, but, fortunately for us, they usually accept our offerings in spite of the obvious danger they have felt, though the same danger compels them to take the bait 'hit-and-run' style. (The detection of lines, hooks and resistance is probably the reason why most other fish usually bolt off with the bait.)

You should always take every opportunity to study fish, be they barbel or any other species, when you come upon them unawares in their natural environment. You can learn so much from simply watching their actions and reactions that it is always worth sacrificing fishing time to spend an hour or so studying their behaviour. If you are fortunate enough to have with you one or two baits, and you can flick these to the fish without scaring them off, it is interesting to see how, or even if, they respond. If they do respond you may be able to see if they approach it with caution or with carelessness. Better still, if you are in a position to present these baits on tackle to fish you can see, then you may learn more about fish behaviour in one hour than you would in a season of fishing 'blind'.

One thing you will notice at times when you are watching the barbel is the extraordinary way they flip belly-upwards to take food that is more than a foot or so off bottom. Sometimes, it is this flash of white belly that gives them away when you are roaming the river bank trying to spot them. Trotting a bait down at the same depth you have seen them turning very often pays off with a fish or two.

Another thing I have noticed when the barbel are doing this somersaulting business is that there is very often a number of chub below the barbel. I know that many anglers swear that barbel dominate a swim and force the chub to evacuate the area when they commence feeding. In the general run of life in a river this may be very true, but many times I have been able to take barbel and chub from the same swim simply by altering the depth at which my bait is fishing. Nor has it always been the chub which were taken from the bottom; several times the barbel have been on the bottom and the chub hovering above them.

Barbel fishing in the early days, and I am talking of more than a hundred years ago, was very popular amongst the gentry, who used to employ a man to bait a swim with thousands of lobworms over a period of days, sometimes weeks. In these swims, on either the Thames or the Trent (which were the only barbel rivers in the country at that time) the barbel used to

31

gather in huge shoals which the lucky angler decimated, usually with a trotted lobworm from a boat moored across the river. I cannot help but wonder how much more he would have enjoyed catching those fish if he had baited the swim himself.

Subsequently, barbel fishing went through a slack period when interest was lost through an increased enthusiasm for game fishing. More recently, interest revived when barbel became more widely distributed and anglers began to throw aside the class barriers and choose a quarry on its own merits rather than choose a fish by virtue of the fact that is has, or has not, an adipose fin.

We have now turned almost full circle, but instead of employing someone to bait the swim, we have turned to a choice of mechanical devices which do a similar job. These are the bait droppers and swimfeeders. They are practical inventions that distribute bait along the bottom of the river bed. The bait dropper is normally used independently of the rod with which you are fishing, and the swimfeeder is used as part of the end tackle to which your baited hook is attached.

Before the advent of swimfeeders and the preoccupation with maggots, casters and hempseed, anglers used a variety of baits and methods to make their catches. These included worms, bread, cheese and meat baits, of which sausage meat and luncheon meat were the most popular. The method of fishing these baits was either with a float or some variety of the link-leger. Good catches of barbel, and many big ones, were taken, but nothing like the catches that swimfeeders, in the right hands, are capable of providing, much more often.

Swimfeeders are plastic tubes from two to four inches long and an inch or so in diameter. Some have a built-in weight strip to provide the weight to hold bottom when the feeder is empty, or a means of attaching a weight of your own choice. The plastic tube is perforated with holes slightly larger than the thickness of an average maggot. There are two basic types of swimfeeder; the open-end which, as the name suggests, has both ends open so that you can use deadbait such as casters and seed baits inside it and block the ends with mud or groundbait. The second type is the block-end which has removable lids, one of which you take off while you fill it with live feed such as maggots.

32

The swimfeeder is attached to the line in the same way you would attach a link-leger, with a swivel, ring, or loop of line that runs on the main line. Or you can simply slide it onto the line through a hole that runs through the centre of the 'feeder. It is usually stopped from six to fifteen inches from the hook, but this can be increased or decreased for special situations that demand either a longer or shorter tail.

The purpose of the swimfeeder is, generally speaking, to distribute loose feed around the baited hook. A better description of its use is that it automatically loose feeds the swim with a high degree of accuracy and efficiency.

The usual manner of groundbaiting and introducing hookbait samples to the fish is to throw a handful of feed onto the surface of the river to a spot where, in the angler's judgment, the feed will sink in good time to trickle through the fishing area. The snag is that small dace, bleak, and other small fish that feed at or near the surface, can devour much of this loose feed before it reaches bottom. Again, throwing by hand, throwing stick or catapult, is only as accurate as our individual capabilities and means that we not only have to throw accurately, but also cast accurately—and we must do this in both instances every time we retrieve for another cast. It should also be noted that loose feeding by hand or throwing device almost always involves a certain degree of 'spread'. A scattering of maggots or whatever that hits the surface in, say, an 18 inch circle (which is the least 'spread' you can hope for) will spread far more than that by the time the current has had its way with it and it reaches bottom.

A bait dropper, as opposed to a swimfeeder, has limitations. To a certain extent it still relies on your dropping the bait on the same line that your tackle is lying. It is useless if you are fishing any distance from the bank, or even close to the bank but a distance downstream, for in this instance it may attract fish past your baited hook and to the source of the feed. It is also an independent feeding method which involves a separate rod and line to lower the dropper in, or, if used with the same rod and line with which you are fishing, takes up precious minutes of time when your hookbait could be in the water; valuable minutes when the barbel are mad on feed.

The swimfeeder acts like a magnet. If cast accurately each time you fill it, it progressively distributes the loose feed down a narrow path through the swim. It draws fish to itself, the source, where your baited hook is lying. The essential thing is accuracy, for swimfeeder fishing is not the willy-nilly method of fishing that some anglers would have you believe. Without accuracy you will succeed only in forming several paths of loose feed across the river, which is defeating the whole object of the swimfeeder principle. If you are not using the swimfeeder as it should be used then you may as well tackle up with a link-leger and feed by hand.

You cannot put a time on how long it takes for a swimfeeder to empty. This will vary according to the feed you are using; the type of swimfeeder; the size and number of the perforations in it, and the type of swim where you are using it. Obviously, the stronger the current, the more quickly the swimfeeder will empty.

But when you begin fishing, if it is a swim you have never fished before with a swimfeeder, it is essential that you find out how long it takes to empty so that you can set up a rhythm of casting and feeding. If you think the 'feeder is emptying too fast it is a simple matter to block up a few of the holes with a piece of sticky tape. If it is emptying too slowly you can burn some of the holes a bit bigger with a cigarette end or cut them into wider slots with a knife or pair of scissors.

Once I know how fast my 'feeder is emptying, or have made it empty at the pace I require, I cast very frequently for the first twenty minutes or so—as fast as the emptying of the 'feeder will allow—and then slow down only just enough to keep a steady trickle of feed through the swim. Once the barbel begin feeding I regulate the filling and casting of the swimfeeder according to how well the fish are responding.

Another little trick I use when I first begin to fish the swim is to throw just two handfuls of feed, well-spread, across the river. My intention is to let the barbel in all areas know that there is free feed about in the hope that they will then begin to search for the source. The source, when they find it, is my swimfeeder which I have been casting and retrieving quite frequently since those initial handfuls.

34

I have noticed, once the fish have begun feeding and I have set up a steady rhythm with the swimfeeder, that the crucial time for getting bites is up to thirty seconds after the 'feeder has hit the surface. This is the deadly period when you can most expect a good take. I am convinced that this is because the barbel are so conditioned to seeing this plastic larder pop through the surface and spread good things to eat along the bottom, they are waiting for it to happen.

I have heard many anglers say that they dislike swimfeeders because they cause too much disturbance when they hit the surface, but I reckon this disturbance becomes part of the attraction once the barbel have associated the splash with food. I am so convinced that this is a fact I often only half-fill the 'feeder so that I can cast more often and take advantage of the extra number of casts and splashes and those thirty-second deadly periods.

To prove my point, it is a well-known fact that barbel quite often grab the 'feeder itself, sometimes even before it has reached bottom. Indeed, I have heard of some anglers who deliberately attach a big hook to the 'feeder and catch plenty of barbel on it. There is nothing illegal in this method, to my knowledge anyway, but I avoid it because to me it seems like cheating. I rather suspect it could lead to a lot of foul-hooked fish, which is another thing I deplore when done deliberately.

Having sung the praises of swimfeeders I must point out that I do not think they are the be-all and end-all of barbel fishing, specially for the very big ones. Not that 'feeders do not tempt big barbel, but they are extremely cumbersome objects to have on the line when playing these powerful fish in weedy or otherwise snaggy areas. More often than not it is the 'feeder that becomes stuck when the barbel charge through a thick weedbed or the like. I have lost so many big barbel on the Hampshire Avon, Dorset Stour, and the Severn through this that I have been ready to dispense altogether with swimfeeder fishing for big barbel. But because they are so efficient at tempting big barbel to bite in the first place I keep trying different ways of fishing with them to try to overcome the problem.

The snagging of the swimfeeder itself is not the only difficulty. If it were I am sure we could find a way to beat it, such

35

as having a weaker link to the 'feeder so that it will break away when snagged. No, perhaps the real problem is the fact that we have to use such small hooks when using the swimfeeder with maggots or casters, which are the two baits with which 'feeders are associated. Although barbel are so stupid when they are feeding ravenously, they are not so stupid they cannot learn a few tricks of their own to enable them to feed in the face of apparent danger. One of those tricks is simply to take a lip-hold of the maggots without the hook being inside their mouths, which they do quite easily when the hook is a substantial one. This compels us to use increasingly smaller hooks as the barbel become aware of the dangers, and more skilful in their lip-hold tactics.

The use of small hooks seriously restricts the strength of our tackle. If we need a line strength of, say, 8lb, to enable us to deal adequately with big barbel we are discarding this potential strength if the line is tied to a size 16 hook. There is no hook of that size manufactured that has the strength to withstand the pull of an 8lb line, which is thicker in diameter than the hook itself. The ring or the spade-end would need to be out of all proportion to the size of the hook.

You will meet this problem in its most discernible form on rivers, or stretches of river, which are heavily match-fished. The reason for this lies with the majority of match anglers being brainwashed into using gossamer-fine line and tiny hooks, no matter what the species or situation demands. I have sat on the opposite bank of a river to where a match was being fished and seen barbel breaking line time after time, and the reaction has always been the same: the tying on of a hook of the same size to the same line that barbel had already treated with the contempt it deserved. This has happened when I have been catching plenty of barbel, with no breakages, and the matchmen have asked me what I have been using. When told of my 6lb line, or whatever it was, the reply has usually taken the form of, 'Six pound! I don't carry tow-rope with me.' Then back they go to continued breaking off on match-winning fish with their totally inadequate lines. Where the merit is in such a situation is beyond me. No amount of hooked and lost fish will ever equal one on the bank.

But it is this silly attitude towards using appropriate tackle that is the main factor contributing to the barbel's demand for increasingly smaller hooks. The more fish that are hooked and lost on inadequate tackle means an even more delicate approach is needed to hook these fish again, obviously with the same result, only faster. It is a long term problem of course, but it creates a vicious circle that only ends when you discard the circle entirely and approach the situation from a completely new angle.

The answer is to use a hair-rig (a full description of which appears in the carp chapter), which allows us to present the bait on a fine hookless line, backed up with a big hook with which to play the fish.

If small fish are a nuisance, you will find it tedious to have to keep gluing fresh bait to the 'hair'. One way round this is to tie a tiny hook to the hair and to bend inwards slightly the hook point—enough to prevent fish from being hooked but not enough to make hooking bait too difficult.

I generally fish with a short hair for barbel, about ½ inch, but soon lengthen this if I get a few bites and don't hit them. If it still happens, then try a smaller main hook, which will be lighter and more easily sucked into the barbel's mouth.

Another alternative is to use a bait that can be fed via a swim-feeder, but is big enough to be used on a substantial hook. Sweetcorn and other, similar, seedbaits fit the bill perfectly, and I have had some good catches on sweetcorn on the Severn and the Avon. Other seed baits I have used successfully on the Severn are tares and maple peas, but I have not used the latter two very often and do not yet know if they are going to be consistently successful.

Another thing I have tried, which may turn out to be an even better proposition than sweetcorn or the like, is swimfeeder-fed luncheon meat. What I do is chop the luncheon meat into cubes just big enough for a size 8 or 10 hook and mix them with damp groundbait. Used like this in an open-end swimfeeder you can feed the swim with the same accuracy and effectiveness as you can with swimfeeder-fed maggots. The only drawback is the expense if you fish for long sessions and take enough meat to feed continuously.

The methods described so far are suitable for popular waters where it is a case of choosing a swim and staying put for the whole session, which means you must attract fish into your swim and induce them to feed. We cannot always rely on the fish already being there and feeling hungry too. The swimfeeder and baits suitable for it are ideal for this purpose.

If, however, we have opportunities to fish midweek when most other anglers are at work, or fortunate enough to have access to a good piece of barbel river which is less frequently fished, then the best way of catching a big barbel is to stalk one. We can wander over all, or most, of the river bank and either look for the fish themselves or for swims where they are likely to be. If we spot the fish we can cast directly to them with strong tackle and a big bait, or we can move from swim to swim until we find where a big barbel or two are feeding.

One swim I know on the Hampshire Avon near Ringwood can only be fished on a quiet day, when few other anglers are around. Unhappily, such days do not come too often, for I live a long way from Ringwood and it is a very popular river in that area. But I found a pretty deep hole where an extremely thick weedbed forms a roof over part of it. It is under this roof where some really big barbel lie.

The only trouble is that it lies quite close to a footbridge and as soon as anyone walks across it I can guarantee I will not get a bite for at least an hour afterwards. You can see that on busy days it is just not worth fishing there. In midweek, however, the stretch is reasonably quiet and I can conceal myself behind a clump of rushes and cast a big piece of luncheon meat on a link-leger rig right in the deep hole and let the current roll it under the roof.

The first time I fished it I hooked a very big barbel which I estimated at 11lb to 12lb. As soon as the hook went in it charged across the river into a weedbed on the other bank, where it decided to sulk and play at immovable objects. So I gave him a yard of slack line and decided to wait it out. Within ten minutes he was on the move again but came towards me very fast and swam into the weeds that formed the roof over the hole where I had hooked him in the first place. Pulling at him would only have pulled him deeper into the weed. So I gave him slack line and waited again. After half an hour I was still waiting, so I gave him an experimental pull and the hook came back minus the barbel.

Since then I have done something I should have done in the first place: found a gap in the rushes only ten yards downstream where I can heave into the fish without pulling them into more weed. It is a simple matter of keeping the rod high above the rushes while I manoeuvre downstream. I have had several barbel out of the swim since then, but not yet had another chance at a really big one.

Maybe you only get one chance at a fish like that—a particular fish anyway—and I blew my chance through not planning what I was going to do after I had hooked him.

Serves me right, but it always serves as a reminder too, whenever I fish a new swim.

An 8lb 4oz River Severn barbel Graham Marsden took on swimfeeder maggot.

Bream

A look at the fish

The first thing we notice about bream is the distinctive shape, and we wonder how a fish with such a deep body can weigh so little. A 5lb bream is a big fish, and when viewed alongside, say, a 5lb chub, we are curious as to why the bream is only equal in weight. This prompts us to take a closer look at the bream, so we pick it up and immediately feel the narrowness of the belly where it rests in the crease of our fingers. Looking down at the fish we lose sight of its great depth and instead see how thin it is across the back. Now we know why the bream weighs less than a side-on view suggests it should.

I read somewhere that this slenderness was to allow bream freedom of movement between stems of marginal growth such as reeds, and for many years I accepted this as fact. But the more I fished for bream and studied their behaviour the more I began to question the correctness of this theory, for I became aware that sizeable bream are rarely taken near to the margins. At least thirty yards out is the norm, and very often it is more like fifty yards.

One of the few occasions big bream spend any length of time in marginal weed is the two or three weeks in spring or early summer when they spawn. I am sure their bodies were not designed for a two- or three-week period out of the fifty-two weeks in a year, however important that period may be.

I feel certain the purpose of the slimness stems from the natural instinct to shoal in a compact body. Imagine for a moment what easy pickings a huge shoal of small bream are to a pack of marauding pike. Because of the slimness of their bodies it means a shoal of bream, particularly when resting between feeding times, can pack quite tightly together and become a much smaller target than they would present if rotundly shaped. Not only that, but the compactness also means the bream are surrounded by an almost unbroken 'fence' of lateral lines; a natural radar system to provide an early warning of an impending attack. The circle of radar is especially useful when you consider that most of their lives are spent in open water.

The shape of bream, and the size and shape of their fins, can teach us a lot about their way of life. The dorsal fin is like a yacht sail; tall and similarly shaped. On the belly, reaching towards the tail-end of the fish is the anal fin. This anal fin is extremely long, having from twenty-six to thirty-one rays. The great depth of the body, lacking the rotundity found in other species, would make the bream a very ungainly fish without these exceptionally long fins on the back and belly to balance, stabilise and allow it to swim on an even keel.

These facts go a long way towards explaining why the bream is not generally recognised as a hard-fighting fish. The relative thinness of the body lacks strength, and the great depth, even with the stabilising dorsal and anal fin, cause it to be too easily thrown off balance. The initial thump when the hook drives home, and the first short, sharp run are strong enough, but that, usually, is all, at least in comparison to cylindrically-shaped fish. The only other thing you have to be wary of when playing bream is their ability, whether intentional or otherwise, to glide in an arc on the end of your line rather like a kite in a strong wind. If you do not flip him off balance he can quite easily crash right into the marginal weed some distance along your own bank.

The exceptionally deep body also gives us an indication of the action of a bream when feeding, and this knowledge will help tremendously when interpreting the action into terminal rigs and the timing of striking the hook home.

Because the body is deep it means the bream cannot simply sidle up to a bait, suck it into its mouth and move on, all in one motion. What happens is this: it is swimming along on a near-horizontal plane when it spots a morsel of food, which it can see

41

A 9lb 3oz bream taken by Graham Marsden from a Cheshire mere.

quite comfortably directly below it in shallow-enough water because its eyes are tilted downwards to allow for this facility. On sighting the item it gives a flick of the tail and anal fin and tilts towards it.

How close it approaches a food item is dependent on several factors, because the bream, in common with other bottom feeding fish, has the facility of extending lips which it uses to suck and blow a food item to clean it before consuming it. A heavy bait, therefore, has to be tackled from a shorter range than does a light one; a comparatively clean bait—a worm for instance, lying on sand or gravel—has only to be 'vacuumed' a few times, if at all, before the bream swallows it. But a piece of bread lying in almost liquid mud will demand a more prolonged cleaning process.

When a bream sucks a bait to its lips the unwanted material is taken into the mouth and filtered off through the gills. At the end of the suck the lips close momentarily and often the bait is inside the mouth when this happens. If the strike has been timed to perfection—that split second before the bait is ejected—then the fish is usually hooked. The strike, however, can very rarely be timed to such an accurate degree.

This is why, with baits that differ in size, weight, and where on the bottom they lie in regard to cleanliness, we have to use various permutations of length of bite indication, that is to say, the amount of free line we allow it to take before striking. Two or three maggots on a small hook lying on clean sand may only require an indication of an inch or two before the strike can be made. A piece of bread flake on a muddy bottom may need a foot or more, and the indication allowed to yo-yo several times before we can be anywhere near sure of hitting them. Yet again, a big, comparatively heavy bait such as a lobworm, on a clean bottom may require only a few inches, for the sheer weight of this bait means the bream has to position himself quite close to it for the suck to be effective. There are circumstances, of course, when the bream will dispense entirely with vacuuming and simply mouth the bait straight off the bottom. Knowing well a water and its bream, and the way they treat different baits in different conditions in different swims is the only reliable answer. Even then, bream being bream, one cannot always be sure.

Shoals

Bream are strictly shoal fish, and the size of a shoal depends upon many things, but it can generally be taken that the bigger the bream the smaller the shoal.

In waters where bream breed prolifically, spawning every season to a lesser or greater extent, the shoals of small bream— skimmers as they are commonly called—can run into thousands. In due course the numbers will be drastically reduced by natural mortalities, disease and predators being the chief causes. Even then a shoal can be many hundreds strong. These are waters which do not, as a rule, produce big bream, for with so many mouths to share the available food there is only enough to maintain them at a low body weight. The stronger fish will perhaps reach 4lb.

Then there are waters which do not provide the same good spawning facilities; maybe a lack of shallows and plant life in which to lay eggs and milt. Here we may find the bream average 5lb or so, with a top weight of around 7lb. The shoals could still number a hundred or so.

Next we have fisheries, such as the Cheshire meres, which are ideal environments for producing really big bream. Lack of, and inadequate spawning sites; an abundance of rich, natural food; and a good head of predators—usually eels—to prey on what little spawn is laid, is the necessary formulae. The fortunate survivors find themselves with a wealth of food and very little competition in which to grow to their maximum potential.

The shoals rarely exceed fifty, and are more likely to number less than thirty. In later years, when natural mortalities and old age have taken their toll, we may find the shoal is reduced to a dozen fish or fewer. But these will be the veritable monsters; a small, compact shoal of double-figure bream which have to be located with absolute precision before we stand any chance of catching them.

Bream shoal together according to size. Very rarely will you catch a bag of bream of various individual weights. If you are steadily catching 4lb and 5lb bream it is wishful thinking to hope that the next one will be an 8-pounder. And, of course, it applies the other way too. If you are catching 7lb and 8lb fish you have little chance of catching anything under 6lb at that time. There are occasions when you get an odd fish that weighs a couple of pounds more or less than the average on that day, but to expect this to happen is foolhardy. If you are catching 6-pounders and want to catch 8lb bream, then move to another swim, or fish that swim at a different time. It is the only sure way—as long as the water holds bigger bream.

This shoaling in like sizes is established at a very early age, and there is good reason for it. Bream have strong predatory instincts (more of this later) and it would not be safe for bream of only 2 or 3 inches to join a shoal of bigger bream.

There are some bream waters which have poor spawning grounds and a lack of natural food to enable the existing stock to put on excess weight. This is where you find that no matter where and when you fish on that water, the bream are so alike in size that catching them becomes tedious after a while.

One such water is Hitae Loch in Scotland. I used to fish there with some friends several years ago and we rarely caught less than 100lbs in a session. Every one of the bream we caught weighed within 2oz of 4lb, the biggest at 4lb 2oz and the smallest at 3lb 14oz. It was like pulling them off a duplicating machine, and after a while, when we realised we had little or no chance of catching anything bigger, it became so boring we never went again.

The poor spawning facilities were responsible for the lack of smaller bream, and the lack of an excess of natural food made sure a successful brood did not grow to specimen weight. Poor spawning sites *and* an abundance of food is the combination for giant bream; one is practically useless without the other.

A shoal of bream, whatever the size of individual fish or number of fish in a shoal, behave as one. I cannot do better than compare a shoal of bream to a troop of soldiers: a compact, neat, orderly and efficient body of fish that patrol a water when the business of feeding is foremost in their minds.

This affinity of a shoal of bream to a troop of soldiers can be taken a stage further. Every troop has a leader and, putting it simply, the leader uses his initiative and the troops under him behave according to his directives and examples. I am not saying that a bream leader dishes out orders to his underlings in the same way that an army commander does. The leader of a bream shoal merely leads the way and sets a pattern of behaviour that the rest of the shoal follow. Where he goes, and what he does, the rest do likewise.

I have watched a shoal of bream in shallow water for many hours. I had a clear view of them from a branch of a tree that overhung the water, and I watched them on several occasions. There were sixty-three of them. This shoal of bream had a leader; the same leader each time I saw them. I could identify him easily because he was the only two-tone bream in the shoal.

The fact that he was a two-tone fish probably had nothing to do with his leadership. Nor did his size, for he was no bigger (about 5lb) than many of the other bream in the shoal. Why he was chosen as leader I do not know, or if in fact a leader is chosen or simply assumes command. Perhaps, and more likely, he was a particularly aggressive fish.

Watching the shoal from the tree was a revelation. The only disappointment was that I never did see them feeding, for I could have learned such a lot in those short but interesting hours. I have seen individual bream feeding, with the rest of the shoal out of sight, but never part of a shoal feeding together. The shoal I observed from my perch on the tree did not swim in any particular formation. At times the leader was flanked by several fish on either side, but more often than not he was in front by a length or more. Every move he made was duplicated by the rest of the shoal at exactly the same speed and with absolute precision.

It was necessary for me to ensure that this fish was in fact leading the others. I found how to do this by accident. I had taken a couple of slices of bread up the tree with me, with the intention of feeding small pieces of pinched flake into their midst to see if they would accept them. They wouldn't. But when these small knobs of hard bread landed over the leader's head he would veer to one side with the rest of the shoal following, to a fish, a split second after. If the pinches of flake were thrown over any other bream's head then that fish would veer to one side, but only the bream immediately alongside him would react, and then only to get out of the way. When the bread balls hit the water over a bream that was near to the leader, then the leader would react *after* that fish and then, and only then, would the remainder of the shoal follow suit.

46

I did this simple but effective experiment many times over several days. It confirmed, and I had long suspected as much, that bream do in fact have a leader. I sometimes wonder what happens to the rest of the shoal when the leader is caught and retained in a keepnet. Do they go into some kind of limbo; leaderless, lost and lacking direction? Or does another fish quickly take over and assume command?

Could this be the reason why, at times, when we are compiling a good catch, the fish suddenly go off; as suddenly as switching off an electric light? Could we have possibly caught the leader, leaving the shoal bewildered and with sudden loss of appetite?

Patrols

Every bream water has at least one set of imaginary tram-lines which a shoal of bream—or the tram, to maintain the metaphor—follow religiously. These routes, or patrols, are known in bream fisher's jargon as 'beats'. They are invisible paths along the bottom of a fishery which the bream have chosen as their feeding routes, and they adhere to them as though every other area of the water was barren.

The beats are almost always found well out from the margins. Fifteen yards can be taken as a minimum, and forty yards to fifty yards as an average. They do not cover any particular area of the lake bed, but generally take in both deep and shallow water, where both are found. Nor do they follow any specific pattern on the bottom, such as circles or straight lines. They can take any shape and cover vastly varying distances.

The width of the beat will, of course, depend on the size of the shoal. A shoal of small bream that runs into many hundreds will cover a lot of lake bed, possibly as much as fifty yards. A small shoal of big bream may patrol a beat no wider than five yards.

Why bream beats are most often quite some distance from the margins is difficult to say. I feel certain, however, that it has something to do with predators; the human kind included. I am sure they feel much safer in open water, where their surrounding radar system of lateral lines can be used to utmost effect. The usual lairs of sniping pike, marginal rushes and other bankside vegetation, are too much of a threat to their comfort. I am sure too, that this safety-first instinct has a lot to do with the fact that big bream are rarely caught from small bays, those semi-circular enclosures which are so appealing to the angler's eye, and such deadly traps for the use of a pack of predators. Because really big bream are too much of a mouthful for even the biggest pike does not mean that a big bream has lost its natural, cautious instinct. An increase in size means an increase in caution, logical or not.

Rolling bream

When bream patrol their feeding routes they frequently display themselves at the surface. The frequency and extent of the roll varies from day to day and from one set of conditions to another. The usual roll can be likened to the surface activity of a porpoise; a smooth, slicing motion, where the top of the head, then the humped back, and finally the tip of the caudal fin, cut through the water with considerable elegance and beauty.

When bream are rolling in this manner it is quite easy to miss them if your eyes are not glued to the water all the time. The action is so smooth and the water displacement so little, hardly any evidence of a disturbed surface, even in calm conditions, remains. Bream do not always roll so smoothly though. There are times when they almost entirely break surface and re-enter the water with a resounding slap of their tails.

At the other end of the scale they quite often roll just beneath the surface, and if the water is choppy you will not know it is happening. If the surface is calm, and you are watching carefully, preferably with binoculars, you will see a slight vortex at the surface due to the water displacement beneath. Sometimes you may spot an occasional dorsal fin when it pops out like a miniature yacht sail.

I have deliberately refrained from referring to the movement as a 'pre-feed' roll, as it is commonly termed. It is inaccurate, for it implies that bream roll only before feeding. This is quite untrue, for bream roll both during and after feeding, as well as before feeding.

That the rolling performance has some connection with feeding there is no doubt, but to what extent is difficult to say. I have heard it said that when bream break surface it is simply to obtain the extra oxygen available there. This could well be so, but an increase in oxygen is coincident with an increase in appetite, so one could well go with the other.

What clouds the issue is that I have caught hundreds of bream, of all sizes, and from a variety of waters, when the surface of the water has not been broken once by a fish. I also know of several productive bream waters where the bream never show themselves at all until they are being brought to the landing net. I often wonder if the rolling activity at such times is happening well below the surface; so far below that there can be no visible signs of disturbance, even in calm water. I cannot say with any degree of certainty that this is happening, but the rolling performance is part of the bream's basic instincts, and therefore I cannot believe that certain members of a species abandon entirely a basic behavioural activity. I feel sure they must be rolling in the upper layer of water where there could be more dissolved oxygen than in the lower layer, but so far below surface there is no visible evidence.

If this is true, then why don't they roll right at the surface like 80 per cent of other bream? I cannot pinpoint any appreciable difference between the 'non-rolling' bream waters and the 'rolling' ones. It is a veritable enigma, and the answer to it would probably not put more fish into my net, but would greatly satisfy my curiosity.

Nevertheless, the greater majority of bream waters hold bream that do roll at the surface sometime in the course of feeding. We can use this knowledge to our advantage when trying to locate the beats. But we must be sure that what we are seeing is a true feeding roll and not just any surface activity, for bream do frequently appear at the surface when feeding is far from their thoughts.

A true feeding roll is always performed in the same direction by each rolling bream. Whichever direction the bream are following, it is in that direction the bream will roll. When a big shoal is feeding dozens of bream can be seen rolling at the same time, all facing the same way. As fish are sinking back through the surface, other fish will be appearing through it, so that there is constant activity. It is as though the bream were connected to sticks with several people stood on the bottom pushing one fish up as they pull another one down. When the fish are very big, and the shoal small, only one or two bream will make an appearance at any given time. But do not judge the size of a shoal by the number of fish you see rolling, for it could be a big shoal with just a few fish rolling, or a small shoal with all the fish rolling.

If ever you see bream at the surface moving in several different directions, or merely lying with their backs or just the tip of their dorsal fins out of the water, or cruising sedately along, then they are not rolling or feeding bream. Do not make any judgments from bream behaving in this way, for they can mislead you as to where the beat is. When bream are resting they can be anywhere, and usually anywhere but where the patrol route is.

Bream layers

There is a popular theory that bream shoal in layers. That is, you can have a shoal of bream of one size at or near the bottom of a water, and a shoal of bigger or smaller bream above them.

It was Peter Stone who popularised the theory, and then went on to prove its validity by float fishing at different depths and catching big bream from one depth and smaller ones from another depth. So for me, bream layers do exist, if only in rivers, for Peter says he has yet to prove whether they exist in stillwaters.

I do not believe they do exist in stillwaters, for I am sure I would have found some evidence of the layer theory during the time I have been catching hundreds of stillwater bream. I have caught fish 'on the drop' with leger tackle, and I have experimented with float tackle at different depths, but I have never found the slightest evidence of bream shoaling in different size layers in stillwaters. For the sake of discussion, however, let us assume that bream layers are a fact in rivers and non-existent in stillwaters. Let us ask ourselves why this should be so.

Remember that most shoals of sizeable bream, say fish of more than 3lb, patrol beats well out from the banks. The only place that is well out from the banks on a river is the middle

Graham Marsden slips an 8lb bream back into the mere.

section. If a stretch of river holds more than one shoal of bream that patrol the same beat, then the only way they can pass each other when feeding on the same beat at the same time, is for one shoal to pass over the other. It is very unlikely that the shoals would mix, for each shoal, once it is established, becomes a very individual, self-contained unit which does not allow outsiders into its ranks.

It may be that in rivers there are times when two or even more shoals rendezvous at a point along a shared beat and pass each other—whether travelling in the same direction or not—by swimming over the top of whoever has arrived first. When these shoals meet it is very likely to occur over a groundbaited area which has stopped one shoal in its tracks, and the other shoal pauses over the top to intercept the crumbs which are sent swirling upwards from the feeding shoal on the bottom.

The situation does not occur on stillwaters because there is enough water well out from the banks to allow the beats to be separated, if only by a few yards. There is also plenty of water for the shoals to be feeding at the same time in widely separated places. It is true, too, that it is easier to harvest a large netful of bream from a river than it is from a stillwater. The fact that several shoals are compelled by circumstances to amass in a swim at the same time may be the explanation as to why it is easier to make a big catch from a river.

The only time you will find bream layers in stillwaters is in small or narrow lakes and canals where there is too little room for more than one beat, and small waters are not suitable for growing big bream anyway.

Choosing the right water
Most quality bream waters have at least three things in common. They are fifteen acres or more in size; they are under-stocked—compared with other waters; and there is an abundance of natural food. To say they are under-stocked is perhaps somewhat inaccurate. It may be more true to say that they are not over-stocked, which is a different matter entirely. They contain the right number of fish, of any species, and maintain this correct balance over a number of years, enabling the residents to grow to their maximum potential size.

One of the few times you will find big bream in waters which do not match up to the points I have mentioned is when they are the result of a recent stocking operation. But the enrichment of the water with such an injection of quality fish does not last long, for the new residents suffer from disorientation and malnutrition. Soon after, perhaps only a matter of weeks, they are dead, or dwindling rapidly in size as they absorb their own body fats. Bream do not transfer successfully even to a water equally as rich as the one they came from.

Some of the most famous big bream waters in Britain are the Cheshire and Shropshire meres. They are rich in natural food and do not encourage over-breeding. Flooded gravel pits and huge reservoirs are also ideal environments for big bream, notably the Tring group of reservoirs in Hertfordshire, and the Oxford T.C. Pit and Queenford Lagoon.

I am convinced, however, that there are many more big bream waters dotted about the country than we suspect. Even in Cheshire, neighbouring Shropshire and Staffordshire, home of the current British record of 16lb 6oz, previously unknown sources of these fish are discovered quite often.

It is true that the quality of most waters runs in cycles; a few years of mediocre fish followed by a few years of quality fish. This is because every so often the fish enjoy a particularly good spawning year, when temperatures, spawning facilities, and lack of interference from predators all contribute to an abundance of surviving spawn and fry. The following years are the period in the cycle that produce bags of medium-sized fish. A spate of poor spawning years eventually produces the big fish period in the cycle.

What I look for when searching for a 'new' big bream water are the points I have mentioned: fifteen or more acres of water, and rich feed. The waters to pay particular attention to are the ones which have produced bream in the past, even big bags of medium-sized fish, but have produced nothing like it in recent years. Very often you will find that the bream have not disappeared entirely, but that the stocks have diminished to such an extent only a comparative few bream are left to enjoy the rich pickings. These remaining few have invariably grown much larger than was previously possible when there was so much competition for the available food.

Once a water has attained this excellent balance of only relatively few big bream, it is surprising how long it can maintain the balance for a number of years afterwards.

Locating the patrol routes
Visual vigilance are all you need to locate the beats on waters where bream frequently roll at the surface. The best time of all to visit a water is one hour before dawn to an hour after the sun has risen. This is the time when bream roll most often.

Choose a spot on the water which gives you a complete view of the whole area of the lake. Take a pair of binoculars with you so that when you spot surface activity in a distant area you can use them to confirm or otherwise that it is bream which are the cause. Make sure, too, it is a feeding roll you are seeing and not any other kind of activity—though it is unlikely to be anything other than a feeding roll at that time of day. Take particular note of every spot you see a bream roll, and after a few visits you will

53

be able to form an accurate picture of where, how long, and what pattern the route forms.

Although it is possible to take bream from most areas along their beat, there are areas, known as hotspots, which are infinitely more productive than anywhere else. There is usually some characteristic along the route—perhaps a ledge or an especially rich bed of bloodworms—which has a special attraction, but quite often it is a turning point, or the terminal point, of a beat which is the hotspot.

When you have noted the area where the bream cease to roll and do not appear again in the immediate vicinity, the terminal point will be a few yards further along in the direction they were travelling. If you see that they cease rolling and then begin rolling again some yards away in a different direction, then the area between the change is the turning point. The terminal or turning point are the areas where you should begin to search for the hotspots.

On waters where the bream are not seen to roll, location is decidedly more difficult, and the areas to begin trial and error experiments will vary from one water to another.

In lakes which have both deep and shallow water, with a distinct shelf that divides the two, then this is a good place to begin. In any event, your first priority should be to plumb the depths of the lake, taking note of ledges, holes, ridges, hard- and soft-bottomed areas, and any other features that could prove attractive to bream.

There are some waters that lie in valleys where the wind has little if any influence on the water, apart from a scurrying ripple that makes little difference to the temperature layers, dissolved oxygen, or food distribution. But in open, or partially open waters, where a wind is capable of creating a choppy surface and influencing the below-surface conditions, it is wise to fish into the wind.

More often than not, an east or north-east wind is cold and detrimental to good fishing, so you will invariably find that you will do better fishing into a west or south-west wind, particularly where attractive bottom features can be reached from the north or north-east bank. However, to say that one bank, or one wind direction, is always better than another does not make much sense. All other things must be equally attractive.

Preparation and pre-baiting
How much preparation is needed depends on the water. Very often the swim you have chosen will not need any modification whatsoever, but on lakes where the banks are swampy and surrounded by a wide belt of rushes some preparation in the close season is necessary.

Obviously, cutting or breaking down a path through the rushes and laying planks over the swampy ground is the first priority. When you have made safe access to the margins you must then decide whether to simply lay a number of planks to take a chair and your tackle, or to be more elaborate and build a proper stage.

My way would be to lay planks and make do with these until I had confirmed that it was in fact a good swim. Then I would build a stage. Planks laid over the flattened rushes restrict your movements to a great extent, for any small, sudden movement is greatly exaggerated by the planks over the unstable, boggy ground. A stage with four or six legs, holding the platform about 2½ft above the surface to allow for fluctuations in water level, is far better in the long term. It is more comfortable and less likely to transmit movement through the water, although great care should still be taken.

Pre-baiting for big bream is essential. Remember that bream, in order to grow big, live in waters rich in natural food, and pre-baiting is necessary to wean them off it enough to accept your offerings.

Free feed in this instance is not to attract them to our swim, for if we have chosen wisely we will already be fishing on the patrol route which they follow regardless of groundbait being present or not. Regular pre-baiting is needed to teach the bream that there is a tasty alternative to bloodworms, daphnia, crustacea, edible plant life, and other items that constitute natural aquatic food.

In order to educate bream the alternative food should be readily available. It is no use whatsoever introducing bait at irregular intervals, for the lesson we are trying to teach them will not sink in if we give them time to forget in between each baiting session. Bait should be introduced as often as possible, at least every other day, but every day is much more effective. In fact, if I had the time and money I would pre-bait every morning and evening.

Doug Sturmey and Graham Marsden hold bream of 9lb 4oz and 9lb 3oz taken from a Cheshire mere.

There is no time limit for pre-baiting. Mine starts at least two weeks before I begin fishing and continues, albeit less frequently, for as long as I am fishing that water.

How much to put in depends on the population of fish, including other species, for you cannot prevent roach, perch, tench and carp etc., from feeding on your offerings. The amount to use also depends on the type of food, for some feed is more filling than others. This is something only you can judge, but most of the waters I fish respond well to a half-bucket of groundbait and up to a pint of maggots and/or fifty or sixty worms. The alternatives are up to a pint of seed bait, such as sweetcorn, a pint of casters, etc. For other baits, and for different waters, it is a case of suck it and see.

If you intend to night-fish, which is usual in order to fish evening and early morning as well as the night itself, then you should aim to introduce your bait in the evening at least two hours before you expect to catch fish. It is important to adhere to this time on every baiting session. You are in fact indulging in a kind of brainwashing technique which, if taken to its ultimate, if this were desirable, could result in the fish feeding out of your hand.

Choosing the right bait for a particular water is important too. There is no such thing as the best bait for bream, only the best bait for a water. I have often read such things as bread being best for bream, or maggots, or worms. This is fallacy, and simply stems from the fact that the angler who sings the praises of one bait uses that bait, and consequently catches more of his fish on that bait than any other. You can, of course, say that a certain bait catches more bream than any other, but what you really mean is that a certain bait is used more often than any other on the waters with which you are acquainted. If pre-baiting is carried out conscientiously, bream can be taught to take practically any edible matter, but there is little chance of success if almost all other anglers on that water are using something else, especially if it is the same alternative food.

Several of the big bream waters I fish respond best to maggots, but this is only because maggots are continually thrown in by everyone who fishes there. It does not mean that maggots are the best bait for bream.

Practically every angler throws in bread groundbait, whatever hookbait he uses, so it is always a good bet that a bread bait will be successful. On the other hand, where maggots are regularly fed into the water in swims which bream frequent, it very often happens that they take over completely and all other baits, including bread, are ignored almost entirely.

So choose your hookbait, and consequently the bait with which you will be pre-baiting, according to what is used most often on that particular water. You can use your favourite bait, if you have one, when you fish a water which is little fished by anyone else. You can always experiment with alternative baits on a spare rod.

Pre-baiting and baiting on the night you fish should, whenever possible, be carried out from a boat. Since most, if not all, big bream swims lie some distance from the bank, groundbait which has to be thrown needs to be packed quite tightly in order not to break up while in flight. Whatever kind of mix you use to facilitate rapid dispersing when it sinks, thrown bait will not spread anywhere near as efficiently as a loose feed which can be spread accurately from a boat.

The feed should form a circular or elliptical pattern. Ideally it should be laid in a fine carpet and not in higgledy-piggledy lumps that bream can break down to easy mouthfuls. Finely spread bait means they have to work hard for a meal and therefore remain in the swim for the maximum length of time.

The mix I use is 50% white and 50% brown crumb, with enough water to make it light and fluffy. From a boat it can be squeezed enough to get a grip on it, and when it hits the water it sinks in a big brown cloud. On top of the carpet of groundbait I then scatter several handfuls of maggots or casters and/or worms, or whatever hookbait I have decided to use. If my chosen hookbait is bread then I make sure to use mashed bread in the groundbait mix.

The use of a boat also brings another advantage. You can place a marker at the edge of the swim which, at forty yards or more range, is a tremendous aid to accurate casting and ensures that groundbait always goes in the same spot. All you need for a marker is a *Fishing Gazette* pike bung or a piece of polystyrene tied to a stone with a length of line about 12 inches longer than the depth of swim.

Tackle

Tackle for long-range leger fishing, which is what big bream fishing is mainly about, should be well balanced.

The rod, in order to pick up a long length of sunken line, should be a minimum of 11ft long, and a maximum of 12ft or it becomes unwieldy. Its action should be stiff enough to cast accurately and not to 'give' too much when striking, but it should still retain enough of its shock-absorber effect to cushion the resistance of a slab-sided bream when first struck into.

My ideal is an 11ft 4in, fast-taper action rod with a test-curve between 1lb and 1¼lb. Most of the action is in the top half of the rod, which is enough to cushion the strike, but is fairly stiff for the rest of its length to give me good casting and striking. It is not too unlike a match rod, in action that is, except that it is slightly more powerful throughout. With this I use a fixed-spool, skirted reel, and there is really no other kind worth considering.

Line needs to be chosen with great care, for when long-range fishing any faults in the line will quickly become apparent. It should be supple and as thin for its breaking strain as possible. It should have no flats, kinks or frays, and its elasticity should be minimal. Its stretchability should be low to assist hook penetration when striking over the great distance, but a certain amount of stretch is needed as a safety margin to assist the cushioning effect of the rod. An ideal compromise between the two, based on the sharpness of your own reflexes, should guide your choice. And choose a line that sinks quickly.

You could compensate for a too-stiff rod and poor reflexes —reflexes which you need for easing off when the hook bites into a lip—by using a stronger line. But this means extra weight to punch the tackle out the required distance and also a greater effort, which inevitably leads to inaccuracy. It also means that you will very often have to use a heavier indicator because of the increased drag imposed on a thicker line in windswept water.

The line I use more often than not is 3lb b.s., but I would not recommend this to anglers with no experience of long-range legering. A line of 4lb or even 5lb b.s. is safer to begin with. I do sometimes go down to 2½lb, but although I have never been broken on it I never feel as confident as I ought. Every time I have to strike my heart is in my mouth, and although I do not consciously hold back when I strike, I wonder if I am doing so without being aware of it.

I use spade-end hooks in sizes 10's, 12's, 14's, 16's and 18's. Chemically sharpened whisker barb hooks are best, especially those by Drennan or Kamasan.

The weight of the Arlesey bomb, of course, depends upon many things: distance you need to cast, bait you are using (bread presents more resistance than maggots for instance), line strength, and conditions—windy or calm—on the day. I use a ¾oz bomb more often than any other, but have ¼oz, ½oz, and 1oz and even 1½oz for when they are needed.

Terminal tackle

There are two main types of terminal tackle, the link-leger and the paternoster, of which there are several variations of each. A more detailed comparison of the two is discussed on pages 12-13.

My preference when fish are feeding hard on the bottom is for the fixed paternoster which, due to the lead being at the extreme end of the line, casts further and more accurately than any other set-up. It is also a very useful rig for fishing over soft mud and weed. The distances between bomb and hook link, and hook and link can be varied to suit different depths of weed and different volumes of mud.

There are many and varied versions of the link-leger designed to combat the same problem. Two popular ones are the fledger and the balsa-bomb. Each has its disadvantages and advantages, but each incorporates a running swivel on the main line which, when fished in waters subject to algae particles, can foul up and obstruct sensitive bite detection, and neither makes for accurate, long-distance casting. The fixed paternoster has none of these disadvantages and many advantages which are discussed in the chapter on tackle (page 7).

On waters which cannot be baited from a boat, and where swims are too distant to be fed by catapult, the use of a swim-feeder to distribute loose feed around the hookbait is often a deadly method. Where the bottom is weedy (ordinary soft weed, not algae) you can incorporate a cork or piece of poly-styrene into the feeder to keep it on top of the weed (see Fig. 3).

Technique

I invariably use two rods, one to experiment with baits and methods, and to cast in different areas in and around the swim. Some anglers use three rods, but I have found that at least one of

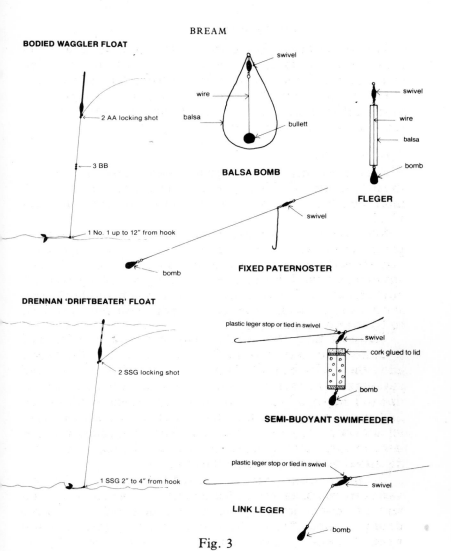

BODIED WAGGLER FLOAT

2 AA locking shot

3 BB

1 No. 1 up to 12" from hook

BALSA BOMB

swivel

wire

balsa

bullett

FLEGER

swivel

wire

balsa

bomb

FIXED PATERNOSTER

swivel

bomb

DRENNAN 'DRIFTBEATER' FLOAT

2 SSG locking shot

1 SSG 2" to 4" from hook

SEMI-BUOYANT SWIMFEEDER

plastic leger stop or tied in swivel

swivel

cork glued to lid

bomb

LINK LEGER

plastic leger stop or tied in swivel

swivel

bomb

Fig. 3

these tends to be neglected. Very often it is this rod that gets a
bite.

My first rod is used to cast to within a yard or two of a
predetermined spot; a spot which I know from past experience
is a productive one. In every bream swim there is one very small
area which will produce more bream than all the rest of the swim

61

put together. If you take special care to note landmarks on the far bank, use a swim marker to aid judgment, and make sure you have noted the exact spot, every time you cast you will soon have this area firmly implanted in your mind. Of course, you vary the cast at first, until you discover the hotspot, but if you have not noted each cast fairly precisely you will not know where the fish came from when you do catch one.

When you catch a fish, or get a strikeable bite and miss it, you should cast a bait back into the water as quickly as possible. More often than not a shoal of big bream, particularly a small shoal of very big bream, does not remain in a swim for long. You should take full advantage of every minute they are present and feeding. It may happen only once in twenty-four hours, and often even less frequently. The bigger the fish the less often they feed.

If you fish with a friend, then begin in separate swims until you know which swim is the productive one. Once you know, then both of you should fish that swim. I see little point in presenting the bream with more groundbait than is necessary, and anyway, if both of you catch fish then you are doubling the pleasure, or if your mate catches and you are unlucky, you can enjoy his success and net the fish for him, which is a pleasure in itself.

At night I use a pair of betalites for indicators, fitted with clips that hold gently onto a loop of line pulled down between butt-ring and reel. Attached to the bottom of the betalite, which is encased in a plastic tube for protection, is a length of braided terylene tied at the other end to my back rod-rest, so that when I strike the indicator pulls off and drops to the ground. This line is also useful for pinching on swan shot when I need a heavier indicator. The front rod-rests hold Optonic alarms.

The only light I use at night is a small torch which I can grip in my mouth while using both hands to bait up, sharpen or change hooks, or make any other adjustments to my tackle. The advantage of not having a light on all the time to illuminate the indicators is that my eyes adjust to the darkness and when it comes to casting or playing fish I am not completely blind.

In daylight I use exactly the same set-up, except that the betalite bobbins are changed for a daylight type that show up brighter. When the fish are well on feed I will put one rod away

Bream taken by Graham Marsden in a single session: 8lb 14oz, 9lb, 9lb 1oz, 9lb 8oz and 11lb 1oz.

and change to a butt-indicator which allows me to fish more quickly and efficiently. This is important when the fish are in the swim and perhaps ready to bite as soon as they see the bait sinking through the water. The butt-indicator remains on the line and is always ready to indicate a bite from the moment your bait enters the water. On such occasions you cannot afford the time, no matter how little, to set up a clip-on bobbin.

The amount of line I allow a bream before striking is usually from nine to twelve inches. Bites usually begin with a slight tremble, or lift of half an inch or so, and then a steady but determined rise that continues until you strike or the fish lets go of the bait. This is the right amount of line to allow a big bream before striking in normal, average circumstances. A big bream is a very deep-bodied fish and would have to stand almost tail to surface to pick a bait direct from the bottom with its lips, which I know they do when they are in that kind of mood.

But I am convinced—from what I have seen and what my commonsense tells me—that more often than not they simply tilt towards the bait at a slight angle and suck it to their lips from distances up to nine inches, a process of vacuuming which they may repeat several times before attempting to swallow the bait. The muddier the bottom the more likely they are to suck and blow the bait to clean it.

Of course, it may be true that bream only rarely suck from as much as nine inches distance, but I always allow that much on the assumption they do. Better, I reckon, to allow more than is necessary, than too little. I do not want to be striking my hook away from the fish before it has even reached its lips. If the fish sucks from three inches and moves my indicator that much, and then bodily moves my indicator another nine inches I am not going to complain.

There are times when it is essential to strike at half-inch twitch bites. This is when the bream are feeding very confidently, usually on maggots which they are picking up directly from the bottom, much as a chicken picks up corn one grain after another without having to move too far to do it. In this instance it is wise to have no more than a 4-inch drop on the indicator and sit with your hand hovering over the rod. An 11-pounder I caught came to such a bite, and four others around 9lb on the same day to similar bites.

The strike should be a firm, fast, straight-back-over-the-shoulder action, with your reflexes alerted to respond to the sudden resistance you feel when you hit a big bream. The moment you feel it you should stop the strike and allow the fish its initial run, which is short-lived but quite strong. After that it is a simple matter of pumping and reeling it to the net.

You should be ready, however, for those awkward bream that decide to use their vast body area like kites. It is just like having a child's kite on the end of your line in a strong wind. As I mentioned earlier, they glide round in an arc and it is a hell of a job to prevent them from plunging into the weeds some way along your own bank. After the first plunge you should endeavour to pull the fish off balance, which is usually not too difficult with these deep but narrow-bodied fish.

I have caught bream which have fought exceptionally well, but these have mainly been fish between 5lb and 7lb from deep, clear water lakes like those found in Ireland. Some bream I have hooked have fought like big tench; strong, powerful runs all the way to the net. But these really hard scrappers have come on short lines when float fishing, and a short line makes a lot of difference to how a fish fights when the elasticity is negligible.

A big bream should be weighed immediately it is caught, for these fish can lose a lot of weight in a short time in a keepnet or keepsack. I have weighed quite a few bream as soon as I have removed the hook, and again several hours later, and while they always lose some weight, there is no specific loss in terms of so many ounces per hour. It varies considerably from fish to fish. The biggest loss I recorded was 11oz in a 9lb 5oz bream which had been in a keepnet for nine hours. The least was 2oz in a 9lb 1oz fish kept for eight hours. Let me add that the latter incidents were many years ago. I no longer retain fish for such long periods.

The only snag to weighing fish immediately is that you should, as I have already mentioned, get your bait back in the water as quickly as possible when the bream are feeding. The best way is to get your mate to weigh it while you re-bait and cast, providing he is not otherwise occupied. When I am fishing on my own I only weigh them straight away if they appear to be over 9lb, and leave the weighing until I pack in if they appear to be less.

When I have a shoal of feeding bream in the swim I cannot rest easy. I am constantly 'working' with my second rod while keeping a watchful eye on my other rod which is cast into the hotspot.

The second, or spare rod, is never left to fish for itself for more than a couple of minutes. If the bottom is not too weedy I constantly twitch the bait along the bottom a few inches at a time. If the bottom is too weedy for this I continually re-bait and cast. I do not cast directly over the swim, but several yards beyond it and draw back to the swim before the bait can settle, covering all areas of the swim and many spots out of it. It is uncanny how many bites I get only seconds after casting or immediately following the bait being twitched along the bottom.

Bread is an excellent big bream bait on most waters, for even when anglers are continually baiting with maggots they usually throw groundbait in too. It is true though, that where waters are absolutely saturated with maggots, even bread comes a poor second.

I usually fish four or five maggots on a 12 hook; two or three grains of sweetcorn on a 10 or an 8. For bread the hook is a size 10 or 8, and for a bunch of two or three brandlings, or a big lob, the hook is a 10, 8 or 6. I sometimes go down to an 18 when maggot fishing or a single brandling or grain of sweetcorn on a 16, but it is not very often such refinements are necessary.

Feeding times for bream, on most waters, are extraordinarily predictable. On several of the meres I fish I can tell to within a few minutes when I will get bites. You can do the same if you note the time every occasion you get a bite or a fish, and fish a water for long enough.

You learn too, which swims are more likely to be productive at any particular time. Some are best in the evening, some around midnight, some for two or three hours following dawn, and others at various times during the day. When you find you have only a few hours to spare you can choose the best swim for that particular period.

Float fishing for big bream
Up till about 1980 I had little experience of float fishing for big bream, and I don't recall ever having read anything on the subject. Perhaps one can assume, therefore, that it is a subject few people know anything about.

It was my view that float fishing would not be a good idea

66

anyhow, for I did not know of any big bream swims close enough to the bank for a float cast. I also considered that big bream were far too shy to tolerate the presence of a punt, with all the inevitable disturbance that punts cause, so relatively close to the swim. A boat is like a floating drum and any noise and vibration are magnified through the water.

In the last few years I have done a lot of float fishing from a punt for big bream and I can state quite categorically that, if it is done correctly, it can be a most deadly method of catching bream.

Before you read any more about float fishing for bream from a punt I would advise you to read the chapter on punt fishing on page 21.

Locating the feeding routes of bream is no less important when float fishing from a punt than when legering from the bank. The only difference is a distinct advantage: on large waters a punt will enable you to fish swims which are not within casting range of the bank.

Very often a bream feeding route will run along the bottom of a distinct ledge, or shelf. Such is one of my favourite swims: the top of the shelf is 2½ft deep and then it rapidly drops away to 8ft at the base. It gives me a tremendous advantage in that I can moor the punt about 15yds back from the top of the shelf, in the shallower water, out of sight of the bream. Another advantage is that a hooked bream can be persuaded—with a little not-too-gentle pulling and guidance—to fight it out in the shallower water and therefore not disturb the remainder of the feeding shoal.

However, the rest of the shoal will not be disturbed too much anyhow, for in spite of what I used to believe, and what many anglers still believe, that big bream are too shy to be caught with such tactics, they will ignore almost anything if you have fed them correctly.

Correct feeding means loose feeding with a so-called multiple particle bait, and in this category are maggots and casters. Casters are the better of the two for the reason that they sink and remain still on the bottom until they are eaten. Bream also love them. The ability to loose feed is a tremendous advantage that fishing at close range (within the firing distance of catapulted maggots and/or casters) gives us. Apart from the lack of noise and disturbance, which balls of groundbait normally cause when carrying hookbait samples to distant swims, there is the added, and greater, advantage that loose feed can be introduced on the 'little and often' principle. A great many big fish anglers think that 'little and often' applies only to match angling when the target is small fish. This is nonsense, for it will work with any species and size of fish.

The idea is to introduce a generous helping of loose feed in the first instance. This will attract the fishes' attention and encourage them to feed. By then introducing smaller helpings of loose feed at regular intervals it keeps the fish interested and, more importantly, it gradually preoccupies them with that particular item of food. Once fish become totally preoccupied, to the extent that they will ignore all other baits, including natural food, they become so intent on feeding they also become almost oblivious to many of the danger signals, i.e. noise and the disturbance of hooked shoal-mates, that would normally have them scuttling to the four corners of the pool.

Feeding little and often with loose feed sounds like a simple exercise that requires no great thought or expertise. However, it is something for which one develops an instinct, or feel, over the years. It is not simply a matter of firing a dozen or so casters into the swim every few minutes; it is a case of knowing just when to step up the feed, when to slow it down, and when to cease feeding altogether.

It all revolves around correct timing, and this depends on the reactions of the fish at the time. Basically, you step up feeding when the number of bites increases, and slow it down as bites slow down. But that is simplifying it too much; for it is like learning how to ride a bike: you can read about the technique, but only lots of practice will give you a feel for it and the essential balance you need.

As far as tackle is concerned, it is very important it is as light as possible and balanced. I use a 2½lb main line, either straight through or to a 2lb hook length. If you married that to your usual 1¼lb test-curve legering rod, you would not get away with it very often. You would break off far more times than you landed a fish. I use a Shakespeare 13ft match rod, which enables

68

me to play big fish on light tackle without undue fear of breakage. Actually, with a match rod and light line you do not really play a fish in the normal way, but rather you guide them, manipulate them, into the landing net. Remember though, you can only do this in open water; if there are snags around you can bet the bream will head for them, and there is no way you are going to stop a big bream on 2lb line.

An excellent bait for bream when the swim is carpeted with casters is one or two redworms, depending on size, tipped with maggot or caster. I fish such a bait on a 14 hook, or go down to a 16 if the bream are being finicky. For some reason bream will still take a redworm even when preoccupied with casters, but there are times when the preoccupation becomes so acute you simply have to use casters on the hook. In this case I begin with two on a 16, and if necessary go down to one caster on an 18. On the very rare occasion I have fished a single caster on a size 20 hook.

I have now settled for two types of float for bream fishing. When I'm fishing from the bank, and the water is choppy, there are few floats better than Drennan 'Driftbeater'. It is an excellent float for beating drift and registers lift bites like no other float can. It is important, however, that the float is set up correctly, which is with a large shot on the bottom. This should be at least an AA, if not an SSG. The shot should also be no more than four inches from the hook (see Fig. 3).

The principle is that the bottom shot holds the float down almost to the sight-bob, then the rod is placed in two rests and the line is tightened until only the sight-bob remains above surface. When a fish sucks in the bait it lifts the bottom shot off the bottom and so allows the buoyancy of the float to take over, resulting in the antenna rising out of the water like the sword Excalibur. It is a wonderful thing to see, and somehow gives you a greater thrill than seeing a conventional float slide under the surface.

When I'm boat fishing I use a plain, bodied waggler, which I shot down to a quarter inch or so off the surface. I use the shotting pattern seen in figure 3. The shot sizes are variable according to casting distances and amount of pull on the water. The shot sizes given are one example only.

Bream weather

One particular weather condition has more effect on bream fishing than any other; wind. Wind has three effects on water. It increases the amount of dissolved oxygen; raises or lowers water temperature; and distributes, to a degree, food. Of the three, dissolved oxygen is the most important factor, but we can ignore none.

Let me describe what I regard as the best conditions of all for bream fishing. The water temperature should be between 60–65°F—the exact figure is not too important providing it is steady or slowly rising. It should be a cloudy night, or day, with at least the threat of rain, if not a light drizzle. There should be a strong, warm, westerly or south-westerly wind making the surface choppy.

Give me all those conditions on a big bream water and I will stand by my rods all night or day.

The worst kind of bream weather is, obviously, just the opposite. Full moon and a cloudless night, falling water temperature and flat calm surface. If I am daft enough to tackle up in those conditions I usually go to sleep and hope I wake up to a change for the better.

There are, of course, many weather conditions between the two extremes when you have a chance of catching bream. Anytime a westerly or south-westerly wind is blowing, for example, means you must be in with a good chance of making a catch, even if other conditions are not equally as good.

A cloudy, but flat calm night, with a steady or rising water temperature is promising too, especially if the night is muggy.

Even in a cold east wind, fishing prospects should not be rejected out of hand if the previous weather conditions have been extremely hot. A lowering of the water temperature, especially with the influx of dissolved oxygen the east wind is thrashing into the water, can be a good thing. This is a case when the west bank could be the best bet, providing the bream have a beat in that area.

In any event, relate the prevailing weather conditions to the conditions over the previous few days, and make your decision of if, or where, to fish on that basis.

The 'perfect bite' enigma
There are occasions, usually occurring when the weather
conditions are near perfect for bream fishing, when you will go
through a period of having bite after bite, all looking perfectly
hittable in the classic bream style—slow and determined—and
when you will become extremely frustrated because you miss
every one.

The first few occasions I experienced this enigma I put it
down simply to the fact that I was fishing too far out and the
bream were brushing against the line and giving me 'line' bites.
I have learned since that this is not always the case.

I have noticed that this frustrating experience usually occurs
in promising conditions when you expect to catch fish, and
when these bites begin they last for unusually long periods and
happen very frequently. To get thirty bites in two hours is not
unusual. Nor is it unusual to miss them all.

What I think is happening is that a big shoal has moved into
the swim; a very hungry shoal of bream that behave very much
like chickens. You know the kind of thing I mean: the chickens
dart into the mêlée, pick up a morsel of food, and then charge
off to eat it in comparative quiet. All wild creatures behave in
the same way when presented with a cache of food and plenty of
competition for it. They move in, grab, and run. The bream
pick up a bait by simply sucking it to the edge of their lips, and
then move away from the main shoal to consume it. All we are
doing when we strike is to pull the hook and bait away from
their lips.

When I first realised that most of the bites were not simply
'line' bites (and you can test this easily by casting in a baitless
hook) I tried every conventional trick in the book to hit them. I
tried smaller hooks and baits; lighter leads; finer lines; a lighter,
or no bite indicator; and opening the bale-arm of the reel and
allowing them to take several yards of line before striking. The
only thing that worked with the odd fish was the open bale-arm,
but more often than not the bream dropped the bait before I
struck. If I struck earlier, I missed it.

The next time it happened I reversed the procedure. Bigger
hooks and baits and heavier indicators brought more success

than anything else I had tried. Not outstanding success, for I was still missing nine out of ten bites, but enough to suggest I was on the right track.

So I asked myself why less sensitive tackle should be more successful than anything else. There was only one conclusion I could come to: heavier baits and indicators were too heavy for the bream to carry away with the bait sucked to the edge of their lips, so they had to grip with their lips to manage it.

The next logical step was to present the bream with a small hook and bait which would be more likely to be right inside their lips when they began to carry it off, but to still retain the heaviness so they could not manage it with a mere suck. A very heavy indicator was tried with promising results. But what was happening now was that the bream were frequently dropping the bait before I could strike.

So I went back to a light indicator, pulled down only a few inches, which was enough to allow the bream to suck the bait to their lips, and then I paused for a few seconds while I watched the line from the rod-tip tightening in the water. Once the light indicator had reached the limit of its travel the bream had to grip the bait to stop it pulling away from its lips. The line tightening in the water told me they had done so, and I struck before all the bow had been taken out of the line. A simpler way, and often very effective, is to fish with a conventional indicator system, then allow the bream to take line against an unchecked reel, i.e. with the reel handle revolving backwards.

It was not the complete answer to the problem, and I doubt if anyone will find it, but it works better than anything else I know. But please, make sure it is the 'perfect bite' enigma before you try any of the methods I have recommended. It may simply be a normal problem which a minor tackle or bait adjustment can deal with. The real thing can be recognised by the incredible number of bites you get in such a short time.

Predatory bream
Bream that eat small fish are not a separate and distinct class of fish, or size of fish, set apart from other bream. All bream, mature bream that is, will devour a small fish as and when the opportunity arises and they have the inclination to do so. This

happens most often when massive shoals of fry from that year's spawning present themselves as an easy meal to a shoal of bream.

Any natural food creature, and you can include small fish in that category, can cause bream and other usually non-predatory species, to become preoccupied with that item when there happens to be an abundance of them. The preoccupation will last until the larder is almost bare.

Apart from the occasions when bream are preoccupied with full larders of fry, there are times all through the year when they will eat a small fish, just the same as there are times when they will chomp a lobworm. You should not fall into the trap of thinking a fish bait is something special; a bait of extraordinary properties that will tempt a super-specimen bream where others will not. There are more 3lb and 4lb bream caught, accidentally or otherwise, on small fish, than there are double-figure bream.

The capture of two 10lb bream from Grafham reservoir on fish imitating lures was treated as though the incidents were especially significant; that lure fishing could be regarded as a specially good method for catching exceptionally big bream. It would be interesting to see how many big bream could be taken from Grafham if bait and bottom fishing were allowed. When fly and lure fishing only are allowed on a water there is no other way that fish can be caught. It does not make lure fishing better than other methods.

Fishing for predatory bream with imitation or real fish should be regarded as an opportunist method to be employed when you happen to see bream chasing fry, or when you have tried all conventional methods and failed; or simply when you fancy your chances with a fish bait.

There will be times when a fish bait will be the best way of catching big bream, but it will never be the best way all the time, or even most of the time.

Black, bronze and two-tone bream

Several years ago I wrote a controversial article in a fishing magazine concerning black, bronze and two-tone bream. It was entitled, 'Do We Have Two Breeds Of Bream?' The title was not mine, and the word 'Breeds' in the title suggested something different to what the article purported to say.

The colouring of bream varies enormously, ranging from a silvery whiteness, through several shades of bronze, to near blackness. In most waters they are the classic golden bronze to which the common bream owes one of its names.

With most other fish the tone of the colouring can be directly related to the environment they inhabit: light colouring in light sand and gravel-bottomed, shallow waters; dark colouring in black mud-bottomed and deep waters. Bream do not always conform to this pattern. There are instances where black, bronze, and silver-sided bream are found in the same water.

The facts are these. I have found all three colourings of bream in light-bottomed waters, in dark-bottomed waters, in shallow waters, in deep waters, and in waters with both dark and light and deep and shallow areas. All three are caught from the same swims, although not necessarily at the same time, and in every case there are two-tone specimens. Whether they are black/white or light bronze/dark bronze two-toners, the dividing line is always in the same position.

For many years it was accepted that two-tone fish (it occurs with other species, but rarely) are the result of winter hibernation, the dark portion of the fish being the part that is buried in bottom mud.

In the article 'Do We Have Two Breeds Of Bream?' I took it upon myself to suggest that two-tone bream are simply another variety of common bream (not another breed) just as black fish and bronze fish in the same water are varieties of the same species, and as mirror and leather carp are varieties of the same species. I have had no reason to change my mind.

Here are two more facts to think about, discovered since I wrote the article. I have caught two-tone bream in winter, and not during a mild spell when hibernation could have been interrupted. A few hours after death a two-tone bream reverts to one colour, the lighter shade.

Hibernation? Parasitical interference with colour-changing mechanism, or simply another variety of common bream? What do you think?

Carp

Carp are a cult fish. There are carp study groups, carp catchers groups, and all other manner of carp worshipping bodies. It is not surprising really, for carp are beautiful fish, they grow to large size, fight very hard, and are not too difficult to catch.

When Richard Walker shattered the carp record with a 44lb common carp from Redmire Pool in 1952 it triggered off the carp craze that dominates the big fish scene today.

No fish has captured the imagination and been dreamed of by anglers more than the carp. The tales of wrist-breaking fights with leviathan carp are legendary, and the ghostly, mist-shrouded waters that provide a backdrop for these real or imaginary scenes only add to the mystique that anglers love.

Redmire itself is one such spiritual water and is the altar where every devoted carp angler would like to worship. It is spoken of in breathless whispers, and woe betide anyone who blasphemes the sacred place. I have not seen Redmire myself, only pictures of it; pictures always taken when the mist is rising, with a low sun providing back light to add to the eerie effect. 'Here is peace and tranquility,' the pictures seem to say. 'Come and fish me, the carp are yours for the taking.'

But Redmire, apart from its almost unique ability to grow exceptionally big carp (it produced the current record of 51lb 8oz), is much the same as a lot of carp waters. Rain can thrash its surface, wind can chop it up, and the carp still have to be outwitted; probably even more than on a water where the natural food is less abundant and the carp are smaller and therefore not so cautious.

There really is too much mystique attached to carp fishing, most of it promoted by anglers who would like you to think that carp are much more difficult to catch than they actually are. Carp are no different than any other big fish. In some waters they are extremely hard to catch, in others they are ridiculously easy.

A lot of the misconceptions stem from the days when catgut and braided nylon was the stuff you tied your hook to; when nylon monofilament was something new and therefore not to be trusted. These days line is, in some cases, less than half the diameter than it was for a given breaking strain.

Since there are more carp and more carp fisheries around today, and so many anglers fishing for carp, it is inevitable that the number caught is higher than it has ever been. The thing to remember is this: modern tackle, fancy baits and productive waters do not make a carp angler. A successful carp angler still has to know his fish. You cannot attack an 'enemy' unless you know where in his environment you can find him at any given time, and the best techniques, properly applied, are needed to bring about his downfall.

Carp are basically bottom feeders. The very nature of their mouths says so. Paradoxically, however, surface feeding is part of their nature too. But it must be pointed out that there are some waters where carp rarely, if ever, feed at the surface. There seems to be no logical or apparent reason for this. A water where they feed both on the bottom and at the surface can be outwardly identical to one where they feed only on the bottom.

Carp are capable of growing and thriving in both small and large lakes. The space they have to grow in seems to have very little to do with the size they can achieve. The main factor that governs their potential size is the amount of natural food and the competition, or lack of it, from other species, and competition from each other. Obviously, the fewer carp competing for the available food the better the chance of reaching a worthwhile size. I have noticed, too, that a lake with sand, or part sand, bottom, nearly always grows big carp. Maybe this is because a sand-bottomed lake does not provide first-class spawning facilities and maintains a well-balanced stock of carp.

76

Climatical conditions also dictate the number and size of carp. The north, due to fewer hours of less warm sunshine, and more severe winters, does not have as many or as big carp as the south. However, our recent spate of hot summers and mild winters seems to be redressing the balance somewhat.

Carp feed on anything edible they can find, animal or vegetable. They will consume enormous numbers of tiny creatures like daphnia, or several large mussels; a large quantity of algae and, at times, one or two small fish.

Carp are not a true shoal fish like most other coarse fish, yet you may see several fish in a group feeding over the same area. This, though, is simply a gathering of independent fish in an area that offers enough food for all of them, such as a baited swim. It is more usual to see individual carp, or just one or two together. Also, unlike bream, big and small carp will feed in the same area at the same time.

Another idiosyncrasy of carp is their unpredictable feeding times. By that I do not mean than one cannot pin them down to set feeding patterns on specific waters. I mean that you cannot say that carp are generally nocturnal feeders, or morning feeders, or whatever. On most waters you have a chance of taking carp at any time of day or night. Of course, there are times when your chances are much greater, such as the early morning, which will, more often than not, produce more carp than the afternoon. Where, say, tench are concerned, you can confidently expect tench in the early morning and know your chances are practically non-existent in the afternoon, which is the case on almost all tench waters.

Prevailing weather conditions dictate if and where in a lake carp will feed. It is not enough simply to take into account the conditions at that particular time. They must be related to the conditions prevailing over several preceding days.

If, for instance, there has been a cold wind blowing for several days and the water temperature has been well down for the time of year, then the wind ceases and the sun brings a sudden warmth to the water, you can almost guarantee that the carp will begin to feed. On the other hand, if the weather is already hot and the water temperature is 70° F. or more, then the wind suddenly springs up and brings a drop in water temperature and

77

a rise in the amount of dissolved oxygen in the water, you can also expect fish.

You can also expect the fish to feed along the shore towards which the wind is blowing. Here, the wind will be having the most effect, blowing the cooler and more comfortable water to that side.

Carp fishing has changed very little in some respects, yet in others it has changed dramatically. The two areas where the greatest change has taken place is in baits and approach. At one time it was assumed that the best approach was one of stealth and caution, particularly as the most productive place to fish was invariably no more than a rod's length away from your own bank.

There are so many anglers fishing for carp today, not all of them recognising or caring that carp can be frightened very easily, it is now more usual to ignore the area immediately in front of you and cast, with specialised tackle, as far as possible. In other words, you do not creep into the 'enemy's' camp, but bombard it from a distance. On many public waters this long-range approach is a necessity, for the dedicated carp anglers are fishing alongside casual anglers who neither know or care that cautiousness and quietness are the essence of good fishing, at least where big fish are concerned.

It is a pity, for much of the pleasure of carp fishing is this tuning-in of a highly developed hunting instinct. To approach a lake with delicacy and quietness, to blend in with the background and, once the bait is in the water only a rod's length out, to sit there with bated breath, using every available piece of cover. It is amazing what an acutely exciting feeling is engendered when you know, or anticipate, that the carp are only a few short yards from where you sit. It is not the same when you do not have to whisper to your companions and you can only dream of the carp as tiny dots sixty yards or more away.

But do not despair. If it is still more important to you to enjoy your fishing, using methods and approaches more akin to your liking, than it is to catch big fish at the cost of a great deal of enjoyment, then there are still a few waters where you can use 'classic' tactics. The carp will probably not be as big as on 'long-range' waters. If they were, these waters would have been invaded before now. A 10lb carp, however, is still a big fish, and if your sense of values is not impaired, then such fish can give tremendous pleasure.

For the moment, let us ignore the modern specialised approach and concentrate on tackling a typical carp lake which will allow you to fish it in whatever style you choose.

It is the coarse fish close season and there are six weeks to go to 16th June. I have found a five-acre lake which has both deep and shallow water and I have heard that it holds a good head of carp averaging 8lb to 14lb with a distinct possibility of a 20-pounder. Apart from that I do not know anything about it.

The first weekend I spend a few hours in a boat making a note of the various depths, the location of weedbeds, and any shelves or basins which could prove attractive to fish. If it had been impossible for one reason or another to use a boat on the water I would have done the best I could with a plummet and noted what I could see from the banks.

The second and third weekend I get to the lake just before daybreak armed with a pair of binoculars and settle down for a couple of hours in a spot which gives me a good view of all, or most, of the water. If I am lucky, and the weather is compatible with fish-spotting, I should see signs of the carp when they push through weedbeds and hump through the surface, or mudclouds and bubbles when they root in the bottom.

At the end of the third weekend I should have an idea of a good swim to fish. I have seen carp rooting in several places but more in one area than any other. I know there is a shelf in the area that runs parallel to the bank about three yards out, and that the water is eight feet deep at the bottom of the shelf. I have seen carp humping the surface over the top of this ledge and even leaping clear of the water on occasions, and at one point along the bottom of the shelf a dense mudcloud was invariably evident.

My next step is to decide what I am going to use to pre-bait with over the next three weeks. I do not see any reason for using anything special, so I choose to bait with two items, bread and worms. Both are as good as anything on a water which is not over-fished.

Ideally, I would have liked to have baited on a little and often basis, say a couple of dozen lobworms and one mashed loaf every day. But time and expense means I have to economise and therefore I choose to bait every other day except for the last three days when I will bait on each of them.

I have already decided that I will fish the water at night, at least to begin with, and this will allow me to fish the three best periods: dusk, darkness and dawn. That decided, I bait the swim every other day at approximately the same time in the evening, for this will teach the carp that there is food available from a certain time. After the first week they should have grown used to the idea that on some evenings the pantry will be bare. But that should not stop them from checking all the same.

On the evenings I bait the swim I spend an hour just sitting and watching the swim after the bait has been introduced, looking for signs of carp moving into the area. I do not see much to encourage me at all, but this does not worry me for it could be much later when they arrive, after I have left for home. Also, one Sunday morning, I took the boat over the swim and stirred the muddy bottom and there were no signs of breadcrumbs in the mudclouds that billowed to the surface. Of course, I cannot be certain it is carp and not some other species eating the bait, but I know it will be fun finding out when the 16th arrives.

There is another job to be done three days before opening night. I need to clear a narrow path through the rushes and also through the lilies that border the margins. I have not done this before for two reasons. The first reason is that I did not want to advertise to anyone interested that a new swim had been created and cultivated. The second reason is that I wanted to educate the carp into finding bait in the area before I alter the character of the swim in any way. Not that I will be changing anything in the immediate area of the shelf at the base of which the bait lies, but I thought it better to give the carp a profound liking for the swim before even one stalk of rush or one lily pad was removed.

I cut a path through the rushes which allows enough space for two rods, and room each side to wade to the water's edge. This will give me a better control over any fish I may hook, for they will no doubt try to charge into the lilies on either side of the swim.

On the eve of the opening of the new season I arrive much earlier than necessary, even though I cannot begin fishing until midnight. But I want to take my time over tackling up and savouring the prospect of the sport I hope to enjoy.

The two rods I piece together are rather special to me. They are Richard Walker's Mk IV design of 1½lb test-curve, but they were very expensive rods at the time I bought them for they are made of a cane called Palakona. I get tremendous pleasure just from handling them. They feel like an extension of my arm, with a sweet action down their 10 ft length which is supple enough to cast free-lined baits and give me a feel of a fighting fish, yet with power to spare when I have to bend it into the run of a big carp.

These rods are designed to match lines from 6lb to 12lb b.s. It is 10lb line I thread through the rings from my fixed-spool reels. I cannot for the life of me understand anglers who use those lifeless, poker-like, stepped-up carp rods coupled with lines of 12lb or less. It is totally pointless to use extra-heavy rods at short range which cannot do the job they were designed for if they are not used with lines of the appropriate strength. What is the point of having an ultra-powerful weapon if it is not armed with the correct ammunition? It is like using an elephant gun to fire air-rifle pellets; inappropriate, inaccurate and completely unbalanced.

Onto one line I tie a size 2, straight-eyed, forged hook, which has been carefully honed with a fine carborundum stone to razor sharpness, and the barb reduced to a bare minimum so as not to impede penetration but still retain a degree of holding power. A size 6 hook is tied to the line on my second rod and this also receives attention from my sharpening stone. The set-up with the smaller hook is completely free of lead, which is known as a free-line rig. I do not need any lead because the size 6 hook will hold a lobworm which is quite capable of being cast a short distance, and able to sink under its own weight. The rig with the size 2 hook, however, is fitted with a very short, two inches, link-leger, made up of a ½oz bomb and a swivel (see Fig. 3 on page 61). I need the weight on this tackle because the bread flake I am going to use will not cast or sink so easily under its own weight.

My front rod-rests are fitted with electric bite alarms and I couple these with tubes of silver kitchen foil as indicators. The

electric bite alarms will give me the initial warning and the silver foil will give me a visual guide to what the carp are doing with the bait.

My large, triangular landing net is stuck net upwards in the mud to the left of the gap in the rushes where it will be handy to get at and easy to catch hold of in the dark.

I place my chair to the left of the swim so that I am hidden behind the wall of rushes and have a good viewpoint of both rods. Around my chair, but out of kicking range, I lay out my bait box of worms, a loaf, my pack of sandwiches, and a flask of hot coffee.

There is nothing to do now but wait, and believe me, midnight seems like a week away. Nor is the waiting made any easier when, at 11.00 p.m. two carp roll over my swim within minutes of each other.

At precisely midnight I lightly prick a lobworm onto the size 6 hook, making sure the hook is only an inch away from the tail-end of the lob, for I have found that I hook more carp when the lobs are impaled in this way. It is wise, too, not to stick the hook in more than necessary to cast the lob without it throwing off. This way it will stay lively for long periods and look much more natural to the fish. Nothing looks worse, and does a poorer job, than a worm which has been stuck on the hook several times and looks as though it has been tied in a knot. Fish do not find worms that look like that and hooks lose so much of their penetrating power.

I cast and make sure the worm lands three or four yards further than the baited area, which allows me to pull it back to the swim and sink the line at the same time. I repeat the action with the other rod, only this time there is a large piece of flake pulled from a new loaf on the size 2 hook.

A tube of silver foil folded over a loop of line pulled down about eighteen inches between bite alarm and reel. I sit back in my chair, full of anticipation and confidence, and barely even notice the chewings and scurryings of rats in the rushes.

At 12.30 a.m. the bite alarm on the worm rod emits its warble and the silver foil jumps two inches toward the rod and then stops. I watch the foil carefully. It moves another two inches and stops, then another two inches and stops, and continues like so until I pick up the rod and strike. I hit into something that feels heavy at first and then comes in quite easily under the pressure I apply. An eel of about 1lb swings out, which luckily is only lip hooked and comes off with no trouble. So much for worms, at least in darkness.

So it is bread on both rods, except that I make a paste for the free-line rod so that I am still offering a bait on a weightless rig. I cast in and try to shrug off the disappointed, deflated feeling that has come over me since the anticlimax of the eel.

At 1.15 a.m., however, the bite alarm on my flake-baited rod shrills out its sudden warning, the silver foil smacks the rod and at the same time I grasp the cork butt and drive the hook into a lip. The reel screams as line is snatched from the slipping spool and then suddenly everything goes slack, giving me a sinking feeling that the hook hold has failed.

But no, I wind as fast as possible and catch up with the fish which is swimming toward me. I feel the resistance seconds later, when the fish plunges into the lilies to the left of the gap I have cut into them. For several minutes I pull and give line in turn as the fish sulks and flaps its tail at the surface. I make no impression on it and all the time I am afraid that its flapping tail will come down on the taut line and snap it like a dry twig. My only alternative is to give it slack line, laying the rod in the rests and hoping it will swim out of its own accord. I do this, and reel my other rod in so that if the carp does give me another chance there will be no other line to get in the way of my landing it.

Within four or five minutes, yet seeming like an eternity, the line begins to peel off the open spool, slowly at first but beginning to pick up momentum as each second passes. I lift the rod and click the bale-arm over with a flick of the reel handle, then wait for the rod-tip to bend.

Knowing that the carp will not have as much energy as when I first hooked it, I pile on the pressure in no uncertain terms, and the fish swings round and immediately makes for the same lily bed it took refuge in previously. But this time I am prepared for it and wind the reel—a fast-retrieve model fortunately—as fast as possible, dipping the rod-tip to the surface of the lake on my right and applying a massive dose of side-strain.

It works, and the fish flips over onto its side for an instant and

I heave desperately to keep it coming. Either the fish is completely exhausted or given no time to gather its power, for I direct it straight to my landing net and it slips inside quite easily. It is a beautiful leather carp of 14¾lb.

But now to reality, for the 'classic' carp fishing days are all but dead. There are so many carp anglers, all fishing with high nutritive value (HNV) boiled baits, attached to hair- and bolt-rigs, usually at long range, you cannot afford to persist with the old baits and rigs and expect much success. Once a water has received a regular supply of HNV baits, and the carp have been hooked on special rigs, they are rarely caught on any other bait or method.

I must deal with baits first, for baits specially for carp have become a totally separate entity from baits for any other species. I thought I would never believe it at one time, but I now accept, along with every other carp angler, that carp can differentiate—given time—between a bait that is no more than a tasty morsel of carbohydrate and one that consists mainly of ingredients with a high nutritive value

It was Fred Wilton who devised the theory that if carp were offered HNV baits over a long enough period, i.e. through extensive prebaiting, they would eventually recognise that they were good for them, and seek out these baits in preference to low protein types such as bread, worms, potatoes or, indeed, even natural food.

Since the early days of HNV baits, however, when relatively few anglers were using them, the popularity of carp fishing and the massive increase in carp waters have rendered prebaiting with HNV baits redundant. Virtually all carp anglers are using HNV baits; therefore, they will be part of the carp's natural diet on popular waters and require no familiarising phase.

The ingredients for HNV baits are available in almost every tackle shop, as are recipes to produce balanced mixes. There are also dozens of mail order outlets where every high protein ingredient, vitamin, appetite stimulator and flavour known to carp anglers are stocked. However, I will not waste space by giving a list of ingredients and several recipes, for the simple truth is that do-it-yourself bait-making is becoming a thing of the past: we are now into pre-packed carp baits, boiled balls of

CARP

various sizes from mini (6mm) to maxi (18mm), preserved or frozen, and ready to slide straight onto hook or hair-rig.

That was another thing discovered: carp seemingly preferred baits that had a tough, leathery skin, which is achieved by rolling the HNV paste into bait-sized balls and boiling them for up to two minutes. Boiled baits, or boilies as they are popularly known, were not devised with that purpose in mind, however, but to deter smaller fish from nibbling the bait away. It was thought that if the balls of soft paste were boiled, long enough to toughen the outer surface, but not for too long so that the inner remained soft, there would still be plenty of flavour left in the bait to serve its purpose, and sufficient toughness to make it extremely difficult for a smaller fish to take the bait in smaller portions. But, the real advantage of a boilie is that it is so tough (the carp do not know it is soft on the inside) that a carp takes the bait by sucking it straight back to its pharyngeal teeth in its throat. It does this with a strong suck and, since the bait is usually on a hair-rig, the hook is also drawn well into the mouth. So, the major reason why the modern carp angler is successful lies with the fact that the boilie, the hair-rig and the bolt-rig marry together so well; they are complementary to each other.

So-called multiple particle baits have also become part of the modern carp angler's armoury. In fact, they became popular before the advent of the boilie. There are many occasions when a particle bait will outfish any other.

A multiple particle bait is any small particle bait that can be fed into the swim in large quantities. The most well-known ones are maggots, casters and sweetcorn. Where carp fishing is concerned it is mainly seed baits that are used for particle fishing. These include hemp, tares, peanuts, tiger nuts, black-eyed beans, maple peas, chick peas, and many others.

Particles in the seed bracket usually have to be soaked and boiled before use. So, please check this out before you use any as bait, otherwise the carp may suffer and even die due to uncooked particles swelling in their stomachs.

Particle baits are very useful when the carp are preoccupied with natural food. Most natural food is found in large quantities of tiny items, so the idea is to confront them with larger quant-

85

ities of small particle baits than can be used on the hook.

When I refer to 'large quantities' I mean only that they are large in comparison with the amount of other types of bait one would normally use, i.e. 1lb of tares represents many thousands of particles, whereas 1lb of groundbait is a small amount. I cannot give you the exact quantities you should use, for it will vary from one water to another according to the carp population.

Any particle should be fished in the same way you fish with maggots or casters: feed a generous quantity into the swim initially, then little and often as the day wears on, the total quantity obviously varying according to how well the carp are feeding.

Most particles can be fished on any conventional float or leger rig. The very small ones, however, such as hempseed, are best fished on the hair-rig, i.e. with several grains of hemp superglued to the hair.

Let's have a look at the hair-rig. All it is is a half-inch to three-inch length of supple nylon or braided terylene (the hair) attached to the bend or eye of a strong hook. The hook is attached to a conventional rig, or a bolt-rig, of which more later.

I have said that this is 'all' a hair-rig is, but now I will describe the principle behind it and then you will realise that it was one of the major advances in technique for many years. With some fish, but particularly carp, a situation was apparent whereby they refused to accept a bait on strong tackle, but could not be landed on tackle fine enough to fool them. What was required was a fine line that was supple enough *and* strong enough to do both tasks.

Carp refused to accept a bait mounted directly on strong tackle because they had learned through the experience of being caught that dangerous (hooked) baits behaved differently from those that were not dangerous (free, unattached baits). They learned that if they blew and sucked a little at *all* baits before they accepted them, the safe ones moved easily and the dangerous ones did not. Obviously, the weight of a big hook, and the rigidity of a heavy line, prohibited movement in a hooked bait.

So, an enterprising chap by the name of Len Middleton came up with an idea that would present the bait on fine, supple line (the hair), and yet still have a strong hook attached to a strong, somewhat rigid line. The hair-rig was born (see Fig. 4).

The principle is that the hook bait is free enough to behave very similarly to loose fed baits, but that the carp suck it in so strongly they also suck in the large hook.

The advent of the boiled bait, not too long before the hair-rig, married very well to this new technique, for it later became apparent that the success of the hair-rig owed a lot to the fact that it was generally used with boilies. Boilies actually encouraged the carp to suck them back to their pharyngeal teeth in order to crush them; this in turn ensured that the large hook entered well into their mouths.

Another problem when carp fishing was twitchers. No, not some fanatical carp angler frightened of someone looking in his bait box, but carp that mouthed a bait and spat it out before the angler could strike—if he'd seen the bite, that is. Twitch bites have always been a problem, and the best answers have been to scale down tackle and bait to encourage a better bite, or to hover over the rod and attempt to strike and hit the twitch bite. Neither method was very successful.

Twitch bites, contrary to what some anglers think, are the product of very confidently feeding fish, unlike the carp that runs off strong and fast with a bait. The 'runners' are carp that have realised the bait is suspicious and bolted off with it in fright. Twitchers are simply moving easily from one bait to another; sucking, blowing, tasting as they go.

It was theorised that if you could panic the twitchers, and turn the twitches into runs, that would be the answer. Hence the birth of the bolt-rig (see Fig. 4).

The bolt-rig generally incorporates a hair-rig, or at least some kind of rig that entails the exposure of most of the hook point and gape. The next most important feature is a heavy weight; at least a 1½oz bomb, but more likely a bomb of 2oz, and up to 3oz. A yard or so up the line from the bomb a swivel or ring is tied in as a back stop.

The bolt-rig works like this: the carp picks up the bait by sucking it into its mouth, but on the outward journey, when it blows to eject it, the hook point (which is bare in a hair-rig remember) pricks the carp's mouth. This panics the fish, which immediately bolts, comes up against the heavy bomb which pulls the hook in some more, and then the back stop hits the bomb and penetration of the hook is complete. Another way is to use a fixed bomb so that the carp has to drag the bomb as it runs, also ensuring the hook pulls home.

You can see then that the boilie, the hair-rig and the bolt-rig all complement each other; hence the phenomenal success of the combined technique.

Another significant change in carp fishing technique has been in surface fishing. Not too long ago there was only one recognised bait, and that was bread crust. This was fished either freelined or anchored from the bottom. Now we have a whole array of baits, which are mainly dog and cat biscuits, such as Munchies and Chum Mixer. What I do is place two or three handfuls of biscuit into a polythene bag, then mix about 20ml of a favourite bait flavour into half a cup of lukewarm water. I pour this over the biscuits, seal the bag, leaving a pocket of air inside like a balloon, and shake vigorously. Do this the day before you intend to fish, and give them a good shake every time you walk past them. If you get it right, and it is not difficult—the ratio of water to biscuits is not critical—the biscuits will turn into lovely, spongy balls of flavoured bait. You can even colour them by mixing a food dye into the half cup of water. They turn out a little patchy, but it does not seem to matter to the fish.

Other baits that can also be good on their day are certain seeds, such as sunflower. And don't neglect casters—they can be excellent.

Techniques have changed to some extent in that there are now a number of excellent buoyant legers on the market which allow anchored floaters to be used to more effect. More significant are the new controllers, an excellent model called a 'Suspender' being produced by Gardner Tackle. It resembles a rather gangly float, being a plastic tube with a ball of polystyrene and a brass balance at one end. What it does is lie at half cock and suspend a floating bait onto the water's surface. The advantage is that there is no line, visible to the fish, coming from the bait, either on the surface or going down to the bottom.

Believe me, this is a major step forward, because carp that have been caught on floating baits before know exactly what to look for. Some are so cunning they can knock a bait off the hook with their tails and then take it almost in one movement. The 'Suspender' gives floaters a new lease of life.

Along with the search for the ultimate magic bait, another change in carp fishing techniques on over-exploited waters is the striving for extra distance. The increase in carp-scaring activity around the banks has forced the carp to feed at the greatest distance from the activity, and the angler who can cast the furthest, within reason, stands the best chance of success. But do not fall into the trap of doing something I saw recently. Two anglers on opposite banks were casting three-quarters of the way across.

Fishing for carp at long range is, on some waters, essential for success. Bankside activity has reached such a pitch, even at night, that the carp will not come near the margins. Distances in excess of eighty yards require special tactics and techniques.

The ideal rod is a fast taper carbon, or carbon/aramid, 12ft in length and with a 2½lb test curve. The reel line should be as light as you can get away with; perhaps as low as 6lb in open water but 8lb is more sensible, specially in the new extra thin nylons. The line should slightly overfill the spool. A shock leader of about 20ft is essential, and should be 12lb to 15lb test.

A bolt-rig, incorporating a 2oz to 3oz bomb, although not essential, is nevertheless a very successful method for this extreme long range fishing. Obviously, you need a heavy bomb to cast the distance, so you may as well use bolt-rig tactics that will take a great deal of sag out of that great length of line when you clip up to the rod. Line clips and foam rubber stuffed into the butt ring are, respectively, a means of applying tension to the line and sustaining it. This allows the carp no slack whatsoever and no opportunity, therefore, to shed the hook.

When casting, I have the bomb hanging about three feet from the rod-tip (if you always keep this distance the same you have a better chance of casting consistently) with my right hand around the butt and reel seat, and the line looped over my index finger. My left hand lightly grips the rod-butt at the bottom. (The reverse, of course, for left-handed anglers.)

I stand with my feet about eighteen inches apart, with my left foot forward of my right so that I can easily swivel from the hips from looking parallel to the bank through to facing my 'target'. I imagine there is a pivot through the rod-butt midway between my hands, like grasping opposite spokes of a wheel with the axle in the middle. I hold the rod parallel to the ground over my right shoulder, with the butt pointing at the target, glance at my rod-tip and tackle to make sure everything is free, then look at the target and keep my eye on it while I push with my right hand and pull with my left. If you make sure the butt points at the target in the initial stages, and the tip follows through in a straight line, you will acquire both distance and accuracy after only a short period of practice. Never try to force it, or you will cast anywhere but where you want to.

In the last few years several books have been written solely about carp fishing. It is not surprising, for there have been a great many developments aimed at putting more carp on the bank.

I have touched on some of these developments in this chapter, but cannot hope to describe the whole picture in detail. I have not even been able to describe all the various tackle items now available for carp fishing. The only way I could have done real justice to the subject would have been to cut down on other chapters, and that would have made it more of a carp book than anything else. I did not want that. The other species are too important to neglect.

Two books that will give you all the details you could wish for on carp fishing are *The Carp Strikes Back* by Rod Hutchinson (Wonderdog Publications) and *Carp Fever* by Kevin Maddocks (Beekay).

I think it is a pity that so many anglers are devoting their whole fishing careers to the one species. Anglers who take this path—usually young, relatively inexperienced anglers who have been drawn into the cultish scene—rarely devote a life-time to angling, as do most all-round anglers. The pity is that they are missing so much; for instance, they will never know what it is like to fish a small stream, or any river except perhaps a sluggish canal-like one. It is not surprising that many give up fishing at an age when they should be at their peak, with a true set of values and the all too rare ability to enjoy themselves even when fish are not being very cooperative. It is not unexpected because an angler with an active brain, as applies to most specialist anglers, has not got enough challenge with one species. There is not sufficient, no matter how good or difficult are the carp waters he fishes, to sustain his interest for a lifetime. And by the time he realises it, his love affair with fishing is over, and he can never recapture that truly magical feeling again. So, think wisely before you devote all your time to carp—or any other single species.

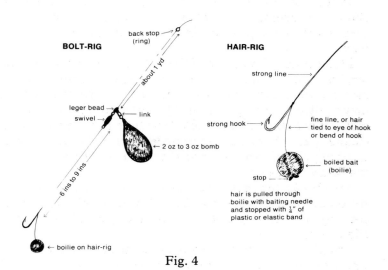

Fig. 4

Chub

I have a very soft spot in my heart for chub. They were the first big fish I tried to catch when I decided to be more selective with my fishing, and when I did catch a big chub on my first attempt it set the scene for my present angling outlook. Had I been a little less successful in catching chub or, worse, met with a complete blank, then Heaven knows if I would have continued specimen hunting. I might have returned to match fishing, which never gave me the same enjoyment, even when I won, that a big fish always does, and, I hope, always will.

In retrospect, I know now that I could not have chosen a more co-operative species than the chub with which to begin a vocation in big-fish angling. If one never forgets that chub are, in Isaac Walton's words, 'the most fearfullest of fishes', then the rest is comparatively easy. Chub are one of the most obliging fish because they are almost always hungry, and their appetites stay tuned, although to a lesser degree, even when the weather is at its most severe at each end of the scale. A big crust on the surface when the sun is beating down will be taken with relish, and a tiny morsel of crumb on the bottom will often tempt a chub even in a snowstorm.

But before you go rushing off to the river to catch a netful of chub, bear in mind that I have said only that chub are easy to catch compared to most other species. Chub do have their days when the old grey matter works overtime and you will have to put on your own thinking cap and go through a whole array of angling techniques, usual and offbeat ones, before you hit on the right one to catch him. Even then you may have to use that extra bit of guile before you have one in the net.

Chub are a confounding fish. At times you can easily 'con' one into your net, and at other times you find they are less gullible. They confound you because there are times when conditions are compatible only to a warm bed yet you end the day with a netful of fish. Then there are times when conditions are so ideal you would almost expect to catch fish on a baitless hook, but the net remains idle.

A day I had on the Severn some years ago exemplifies the contrariness of chub. I took a friend with me who had caught chub only from the river Dane where the average size was 1½lb. On the Severn, at least on the particular stretch we fished, the average size was around twice that weight, and my friend was looking forward to catching a 4-pounder, which was double the weight of his previous best. I, being the eternal optimist, almost guaranteed him one. (I have learned my lesson since, and now, never, ever, promise anyone they will catch fish.)

It was winter and we made an early start, travelling the seventy-odd miles in darkness so as to arrive with time to tackle up and be fishing as the last dregs of darkness dripped away. In the Welsh hills, where the Severn still looks like a river and not the characterless drain it is in the middle and lower reaches, there was ice on the road, and this slowed us down considerably. It was daylight when we arrived.

I proposed that we fish the same swim, which was large enough to accommodate both of us without the risk of crossed lines. The current was strongest along the far bank and gradually lessened in strength until it reached a couple of yards from our bank, where it was almost slack.

I tackled up with a simple running bullet stopped two inches from the size 6 hook. Bait was a piece of crust from a new loaf. I cast a third of the way across and then allowed the current to roll the tackle round until the bait came to rest just on the edge of the slack. My mate was still trying to tie a hook on for, unlike mine, his fingers were numb with cold.

'Come on,' I said. 'The river looks great, we should have a few today.'

I was about to take the line and hook off him and tie the knot, when my rod-tip dipped. I struck, played the fish, and netted a good chub of almost 4lb. I slid it into my keepnet, re-baited and cast to the same spot. I took the line and hook off him and immediately had to drop them again so that I could strike, play and land another chub of about 3lb.

Incredibly, the same thing happened twice more, the last fish topping 4lb. The situation had become embarrassing, so I laid my rod in the rest, with the hook hanging from the butt-ring, and tied on my mate's hook for him.

We never had another bite.

Conditions looked perfect and could not be faulted. The water was running at normal winter level with just a tinge of colour. It was cold but not too cold, and dammit, I had caught four fish with hardly any effort; fish that had taken a big crust with a savage bite that suggested they were very hungry.

We tried every likely swim for a mile up and downstream, combining every conceivable method. It was as though the river had suddenly died; as though a mysterious lethal pollution had struck and wiped out all life.

There was no apparent explanation. The air and water temperature had risen since the early morning frost; the water level and colour remained the same. But that is chub fishing. It had happened before, it has happened since, and it will happen again. It would do me no harm to accept it for what it is: an idiosyncrasy of chub, and stop trying to find out why. But I cannot accept mysteries and I like to find the reason behind them. There is always a reason, and searching for the answer is part of the fun.

The next time you are along the river and you spot a shoal of chub, or an individual fish, see how close you can get before they, or it, take fright. Very often, when I take a walk along the river in the close season and see a shoal of chub sliding in and out of the streamer weed, or merely lying near to the surface, ready to suck in a floating insect, I imagine I have a rod with me and I want to catch one of those chub.

If there is any amount of bankside vegetation the task is somewhat easier than on an open bank. Using the cover of the bushes or whatever, I crouch as low as possible and manoeuvre myself into a position where I know I could cast to them, not forgetting to make a note of a landing site, for it is useless to hook a fish if you cannot play it to the landing net. If it is an open bank then Red Indian tactics are called for; a snake-like slither across the grass flat on your stomach. You will have spotted the chub, or signs of them, from some distance up or downstream, because you will not have been able to approach them upright on an open bank without them spotting you first. When you see them, move back from the river until the edge of the bank shields you from the fish. When you draw level, drop down onto your belly and slide to the edge of the bank until you can slowly raise your head to pinpoint their exact position. Slowly lower your head, slide back a yard or so, and then cast to the fish, or imagine you are casting if you have no rod with you, without allowing the rod-tip to show over the edge of the bank.

It is good practice and you will soon learn how careful you have to be not to scare them—and the bigger the chub are, the more careful you have to be. Remember too, that the chub do not have to see you to take fright. A heavy footfall, the cracking of a twig, or the mere vibration of a toe dragging on the grass while you are crawling on your belly can often be enough.

Walking the river, without tackle, in the close season is a good thing for many reasons. Not only can you practice approaching chub swims without scaring the chub away, you can also learn where to find them. If the stretches of river you fish for chub are those featureless, barren reaches, with hardly any changes in the pace of the current, or depth; no vegetation; where everything is much of a muchness, then you are unlucky in that the only way you can locate fish is to fish for them, or rely on what other anglers can tell you. I much prefer to find my own swims, not because I think I can find better swims than anyone else, but because I get a great deal of satisfaction from being able to study a piece of water, select a swim as a likely chub haunt, and then find that I am right.

Walking the river in the close season, when the bankside and aquatic vegetation has blossomed and the water is running clear and low, is the best time for actually spotting the chub as they go about their daily business. This is the easiest way to locate them if you are careful in your approach. You will be able to see the lush green streamer weed swaying in the current, and if you look carefully, letting your eyes adjust to the movement of the current and weed, preferably with the use of polaroid spectacles, you may see one or more black shapes that suddenly emerge from under the green ribbon, hover for a few seconds in the open water and then just as suddenly disappear back into the weed.

If you are well practiced in a careful approach, having learned the art of blending yourself into the background and moving with the silence and stealth of a hungry alley-cat, then you will soon be close enough to identify them as chub. You will be able to see them opening and closing their huge mouths as they intercept items of food which the current is bringing to them. You will be able to study them at length and note at what depth they are feeding. Are they hovering around midwater, or near to the surface? Or are their blunt heads dipping to the bottom and sucking food from the sand or gravel?

If you find yourself close to a shoal of feeding chub, take advantage and watch. Take in every little movement they make, watch how they immediately gulp down some items of food, when at other times they will suck and blow it out several times before consuming it. Watch how they move right up to a certain morsel and pick it up with their lips, or how they move no closer than several inches to another and then draw it to the edge of their lips with a mighty suck. See their gills distend with the movement and the flurry of pectoral fins that give the subtle shunting manoeuvre. Note how the smallest fish in the shoal make sudden, unthinking darts in the current. See how they grab at objects whether they are edible or not and then spit them out, only to grab at an identical item soon after. Compare this to how the largest fish move relatively slowly, selecting their food with the discrimination of a gourmet; the subtle approach, the gaping of the cavernous mouth that does not, at times, close over the food but blows it out to rid it of foriegn matter. See how, sometimes, the largest fish will hover at the tail-end of the shoal, while his tasters—or so it seems—accept almost every likely-looking morsel, only to leave some morsels alone as though there was something special about them, and fit only for the King. See how the King sometimes lies near to the bottom, feeding carefully and non-competitively, while his underlings vie with each other for the mid-water scraps.

Remember what you have seen when you are fishing. When

A 5lb ½oz river Severn chub for Graham Marsden

you are experiencing a certain kind of bite which you are finding
difficult to hit, try to relate the bite with what you have seen the
chub doing on your close season excursions, then decide from
there what course of action would be best to hit the fish. Do you
need to hit the bite straight away because the chub are
grabbing? Do you need to give some free line because the chub
are sucking the bait in from a considerable distance?

Chub fishing with natural baits, such as slugs, snails, small
fish, crayfish, shrimp, prawn and worms, takes some beating
during the hot, low-water, summer months. Chub feed on them
extremely fiercely, and even small ones give bites to rival a
ravenous barbel.

Big black or brown slugs are positively deadly. I collect a
dozen or so from the dewy grass in the early morning and set off
for a few hours' chubbing, knowing I am going to catch several
fish, providing, of course, the weather and water conditions are

favourable.

The very fast, shallow water, often no more than a foot deep, is the place to fish for summer chub. Here they have sought out the well-oxygenated water where the streamer weed grows thick and the natural food breeds in profusion. The chub flit in and out of the weed like silent ghosts, grubbing for food, seeking shelter from the bright sun, and sometimes just playing around for the sheer hell of it.

I tackle up with a through-action carbon rod, 11ft long, a fixed-spool reel carrying 5lb b.s. line to which a size 2 hook is tied direct. No float is used, nor any weight, for the big slugs are heavy enough to cast the full width of most rivers, and to hold bottom in most weedy swims. The hook should be honed to a needle-sharp point, and the barb reduced to enhance penetration.

You stick the hook through the slug about a half inch from one end and then cast to a spot where the current will carry the slug beneath the roof of streamer weed, then place the rod in a rod-rest and watch it very carefully. The reason you need to watch the rod carefully is not because bites on slugs are hard to see, but because you risk losing the rod if you do not keep your eye on it. The chub take slugs absolutely savagely, as though they have not fed for a week and their very lives depend on seizing that particular specimen. It is as though someone has swung an invisible sandbag at the rod, it curves over so fast and far, and so suddenly.

Many times the chub take slugs so viciously they rip them clean off the hook, and the only thing you can do to improve matters is to thread the line through the full length of the slug with a baiting needle, attach the hook and pull it back so that one end of the slug is lying in the bend of the hook. Then pinch a small shot on the line at the other end to stop the slug from sliding up the line.

Another effective way of catching summer chub is by fly fishing. I have caught chub on wet and dry fly, particularly on mayfly, but my experience of fly fishing for chub is so limited I would not propose to offer advice on the method. I have heard, however, that large, white, moth-like artificials are especially good at night.

Now let us take a step in time and move from summer to autumn, the time when the lush weed is still present and the water still runs clear at not much more than summer level. It is the end of October and the water temperature has dropped several degrees in the past few weeks, the minnow shoals are less numerous and the chub are fighting fit. I am going fishing. Come with me.

It is a river I know well, but a stretch I have never fished before, and when I see it I wonder why. Seen from a helicopter it would look like a little lad's still-wet scribble on a sheet of green paper, winding and erratic; drawn with a shaky hand. Character oozes from it, and I am content to spend some time studying its many features before I set up a rod. I walk upstream; upstream because I can wade to the other bank if I need to and any disturbance will not carry far against the current. I come to a bend where the outside is undercut and deep and the bank is riddled with a conglomeration of sinewy roots from a huge old tree that leans threateningly over the water, its leafless branches almost touching the smooth surface. The blackened roots reach down into the water itself, like the arms of a negro tickling trout. The undercut cave is dark and mysterious but the lightness of the sandy bottom becomes apparent as I look across the bend, the water becoming shallower as I scan across to the inside of the bend.

Black silhouettes move out of the darkness and change into blunt torpedoes, dark and slow-moving as they glide over the sandy bottom. Then, as one, they slink back into the darkness, seeking privacy and safety in the womb of the undercut.

I watch intently for a half-hour, seeing how often the chub move out of the darkness and into the light, and that the time spent there is more or less the same on each occasion. Two minutes is the most time they spend in the lightness, and four to six minutes in the darkness.

I wonder if it will pay to feed maggots over the sand to persuade the chub to spend more time there, and then to trot a bunch of maggots to them. But I discard that idea, for the water is too shallow over the sand and once a fish is hooked the fishing would be finished for a long time while the rest of the shoal got over the scare. I may not even hook a fish, for the disturbance of

99

retrieving a float through such shallow water, so close to the fish, would be sure to scare them. Anyway, there may be some bigger chub in the undercut, content to lie there, feeding on the scraps that trundle round the bend.

I tackle up my 11ft carbon rod again. This rod is supple in the tip, but becomes powerful as it bends towards the butt. It was designed for lines of 4lb to 8lb b.s., but feels best when married to a line of 6lbs b.s. With 6lb line I can bend into a fish and know that there is some bend remaining; that I have not used all of the shock-absorber effect of the rod.

Before I thread the rod with a line from the fixed-spool reel I hesitate and look again at those blackened roots that reach into the undercut. Finesse will not be the order of this swim. No, those roots demand bully-boy tactics; the chub given no quarter; make or break; muck or nettles; call it what you will.

The chub in this river, however, are no monsters, nowhere near appoaching the record of 8lb 4oz. There are some big ones, but a 5-pounder would be exceptional. I choose 6lb line and feel confident that it will be sufficient to hold any chub in this river. Anyway, I will risk it, not because I want to give the fish a chance; I do not believe in giving any fish a chance, I go to the races when I want to gamble. The only reason I like to use the lightest line possible is so that my tackle, and consequently the bait, will behave as naturally as possible. The lighter the line the less stiff it is, and the more supple the line the more the bait will behave naturally according to the nuances of the current.

I want my bait to lie right in the labyrinth of roots, for this is where the better fish will be dining. It will be tricky casting, for I have overhanging branches to contend with, which leave a gap of six inches only between them and the surface for the tackle to pass through. Even if I cast through this gap accurately, the speed of the cast must be faultless too, for the gap between the branches and the roots is a mere two feet: too far and I am in the roots, too near and my bait will not be lying where I want it. Any errors could ruin the fishing, for if I snag on the overhanging branches or the roots, the subsequent pulling to free the tackle, or to break it, will not go unnoticed by the chub.

I decide to play it safe, so I tackle up with a ¼oz bullet stopped only 1½ inches from the number 4 hook. Bait will be a piece of crust about half the size of a matchbox, torn from a new loaf. My idea is to cast as close to the branches as I dare, then allow the current to carry the bait into the roots. The current, although only slow, should be able to do this easily in the first few seconds before the crust becomes totally waterlogged and is still buoyant enough to counteract the weight of the bullet.

I have stopped the bullet close to the hook for two reasons, the first being that crust is light and buoyant to an extent even when soaked, so the closeness of the bullet will stop it from rising off the bottom any more than the 1½ inch distance of the plastic leger-stop from the hook. The second reason is the snagginess of the swim. If the distance between bait and bullet was, say, 12 inches, then I would have 12 inches of line that would be out of my control. As it is, I have only 1½ inches of line to wrap around a branch or root.

I have tackled up well back from the water's edge. I take my combination tackle bag and seat and walk carefully towards the river, then place the seat near to the water but behind the cover of a hawthorn bush. Then I fetch my rod, landing net, loaf and rod-rest. I slide the rod-rest slowly into the sand, making sure it is positioned to that I can sit comfortably with the butt of the rod in my right hand and the tip pointing at the roots.

After sticking the hook through a crust I make an experimental cast across the river, well away from the swim, choosing a dock leaf as my target on the far bank. This is just to remind me of the feel of the rod and the weight of the tackle I am using. I am pleased to see the bullet land only six inches from the leaf. Re-baiting with a new crust I cast towards the branches, but my subconscious fear of snagging makes me cast a couple of feet short, but I decide to leave it and see what happens.

The tackle and bait roll easily along the bottom, too easily in fact, for it was not necessary to lift the rod-tip at any time to encourage the roll. Within seconds it stops and I can tell from the direction of the line that the bait is lying in the thick of the roots. I decide to leave it; perhaps the safest way of retrieving it without snagging is with a fish on the end.

With the rod in my right hand and the line between butt-ring and reel looped over the middle finger of my left hand I wait impatiently for a bite. I don't have to wait long. A steady pressure tries to pull my finger to the rod, so I go along with the movement for a few inches and then strike. I miss it! But I was so confident I would feel the solidness of either chub or root my reactions are not prepared to stop at the end of the strike. The bullet goes flying over my head and lands in the field behind me. My annoyance at missing the fish turns to relief when I realise I am not snagged in the roots.

I change the ¼oz bullet for one of ½oz, re-bait and then cast. This time my cast lands exactly where I want it, just short of the overhanging branches. The bullet rolls momentarily and then comes to rest, but a slight lift of the rod-tip inches it round a little more, and then another lift until I am satisfied the crust is lying just short of the roots.

I lay the rod in the rod-rest with the butt on the sand so that my line is entering the water at 45 degrees. Then I pull a lump of flake from the loaf and pinch off 10p piece-size pieces and squeeze all the air out of them. One by one I toss them into the slow current about eight feet from the roots. Watching the pinches of flake sink out of sight into the roots I only see the rod-tip curve over out of the corner of my eye. I grab the butt, with my fingers curled around the reel seating, and strike.

There is an unrelenting solidness for a split second, and then a massive surge as the chub plunges for the roots. He fails to make it, for I make an equally massive surge with the rod in the opposite direction. He comes away from the roots and I swing the rod over to my right, parallel with the water, to keep him low and prevent him from splashing at the surface. Everything goes as planned and I soon bully him into the landing net, and from there the hook is removed and he is slid into my big, knotless keepnet, where he can lie safe and recover while I try to catch him some company. He weighs about 3½lb.

I catch three more chub from the swim, weighing from 2lb to 4lb 2oz, before the swim goes dead and I decide to move on and try somewhere else. Only fifty yards further upstream I find a smooth glide along my own bank that looks as though it should hold a few chub. I move back from the river, walk the length of the glide and then, after swapping from leger to float tackle on my 13ft match rod, insert myself between two slender willows at the head of the run.

There is no room for a chair, so I crouch between the willows and hook a plummet onto the size 18 hook. Lowering the plummet into the swim a rod's length out I find it is almost five feet deep at that point. I set the float two inches shallower, and then lay the rod down while I spend five minutes trickling maggots down the run.

The float is a bodied peacock waggler, nine inches long, with an all-black body and a white and dayglo orange tip. It is locked with two swan shot. The line has been changed to one of 2lb b.s., and on this I have pinched 3BB shot midway and a number 4 shot nine inches from the hook. I have changed to lighter line because the swim is snag-free and I will be able to trot with greater control with this thinner and easier-running line.

I make several trots down the run without so much as a tremble of the float. So I wet the line with spit and slide the float and locking shot another foot deeper. (If you fail to wet the line you create heat when you slide the float and shot along it, which could damage the line.) Now the float is dragged under half-way down the run, so I slide the float and locking shot three inches shallower and find this is just right.

I lay the rod down and spend another two or three minutes feeding maggots into the swim. Before I try another trot down I remove the two old maggots from the hook and impale a single fresh one, being careful not to burst it with the size 18 hook which, although sharp, is rather thick in the wire for maggot fishing. My second trot sees the float dip sharply beneath the surface about two-thirds of the way down the swim. I sweep the rod back as much as I can in the confined space and, although the fish is rather small at about 1 ¼lb, it kicks up quite a fuss and there is nothing I can do to stop it splashing.

Before the swim dies I take seven fish, all small chub up to 2lb. I am not surprised they are all small ones for a big chub would not tolerate the disturbance caused when each fish was played through the swim. Still, I marvel at how eagerly and easily a chub will bite, considering how shy they are in all other respects.

Before I move on I note that I could have fished the swim from the other bank, although there was no shallow-enough water nearby to ford the river. Casting into the gap between the

A chub of 4½lb taken by Graham Marsden when touch-legering.

willows would have been difficult but I would have taken a bigger net of fish, with a couple of sizeable ones maybe, for I could have hauled each fish out of the swim immediately it was hooked and kept disturbance down to a minimum. I bear this in mind for my next visit and reflect that I am already learning and making mental notes about this hitherto unfished—by me at any rate—stretch of river.

Much of the next couple of hundred yards of river are fairly shallow and fast and would be good points to fish in the height of summer when fish look for these places for the extra oxygen available there. At this time of the year, late autumn, sufficient oxygen is available in all areas and the chub prefer more water over their heads.

Another five minutes' walk and I find a slow piece of water that looks extremely chubby. Especially so, since there is a big dead tree lying half in the water with a huge rubbish raft

104

collected around the trunk. Chub love such places and I feel confident that here is where I will catch a big one.

I study the swim, working out in my mind the best way of tackling it. As I look at the water I hear a distinctive slurp as a chub sucks some morsel through the surface; then I see the rings rippling away from the spot where it happened. It is in the sweep of water that curls around the trunk. I lay my tackle down, being careful not to cause any vibrations, and creep down to the water's edge some fifteen yards upstream of the tree.

From the loaf I have taken with me I tear off several pieces of crust and toss them one by one into the current, which carries them over the spot where the chub surfaced. The first three crusts are ignored, and then one disappears in a tiny whirlpool caused by the powerful suck of a sizeable chub.

I take about four minutes to retackle the 11ft rod, re-thread the 6lb line and grease it well to make it float, and tie on a size 2 hook—a simple free-line rig that should do the job. My chair and everything apart from the rod, landing net and loaf, are left up the bank. Crusting for chub is an art that requires concentration and constant attention to the performance. I would have no time and no desire to sit down, and a rod-rest is out of the question.

I put a big crust on the hook, dip it for a couple of seconds at the edge of the river to give it casting weight, and then swing it into the current. It is ignored for cast after cast, using a new crust each time of course, but I am not surprised for I am having great difficulty keeping the line from bowing, for the current is slightly faster between the crust and the bank. Every time I flick the rod in an attempt to mend the line the crust pulls off course and washes into the rubbish raft instead of curling round the edge of the tree trunk. If I had some weight near to the crust I could mend the line without pulling it off course. So I pinch a swan-shot four inches from the hook and impale an extra-large crust. The bigger crust, once soaked, will give me more weight, as will the swan-shot, and the crust is big enough to support the weight of the shot.

It works. I can control the crust easily now, and on the third cast the water erupts as a nice chub takes the bait. It weighs 3¾lb. I have to wait a while before I get a second chub, but it is worth it for this one weighs 4lb 10oz and fights like a demon. So long did I have to wait, however, for that second chub, I decide to dispense with floating crust and have a shot at legered crust again. That raft looked mighty inviting.

I re-rig with the ½oz bullet and then cast right to the edge of the raft. Down the crust goes and drifts under the floating roof. I place the rod in the rest and begin to feed pinches of flake into the current in a spot which will carry them under the raft. Nothing happens for quite a while, then the rod-tip trembles, so I hold the rod in one hand and the line in the other.

Touch-legering is not necessary, or so I think when the line is snatched from my fingers and the rod slams over from a vicious bite. But I miss it! How, I don't know. When it happens again on the next cast I turn the air blue with some choice words.

On the next cast I touch-leger again, only with a fairly long loop of line pulled out from between butt-ring and reel (see pages 15-17). When that bite comes again I go with it, paying out line as the fish pulls. When all the line is used up I strike, and the solidness that stops the strike in mid-sweep is a tremendous feeling.

I pull hard, but the fish pulls back even harder. The line whistles like a taut bow-string in a fierce gale and I suddenly feel apprehensive. Will the line hold? I pull harder. To hell with it, I'll go down fighting, it will break me on my terms if it breaks me at all. The fish gives a little, so I give a little, which is a mistake, for the fish takes advantage of my generosity and dives again for whatever refuge it seeks under the raft. The next time it relents, I pull even harder and feel pleased with myself when it comes completely clear of the raft. It seems to give up after that initial tug o'war, a common trait with most chub, and is soon safely in the net. A beauty of 5lb ½oz.

On my way home I reflect on the pleasures of a good day's fishing. I am already planning to catch more and bigger ones the next time I come. The next time I will be armed with some experience of the stretch, and experience is one of the deadliest weapons there is.

Crucian Carp

There is something about Crucian carp that robs them of the popularity they really deserve. It could be that they are considered as the poor relation of the giant of the carp family, the common carp; but smallness in a species does not detract from the popularity of roach and rudd, and Crucians are a small species, the record standing at 5lb 10½oz.

They may not be popular fish because they are so easy to catch in the smaller sizes, up to ¾lb, and serious specimen hunters may not consider them as worthy opponents. Nor is their image helped by the way they perform—again, in the smaller sizes—on the end of a line. The manner in which they fight could be likened to the actions of an erratic yo-yo; a somewhat comical affair that neither taxes your skill nor the strength of your tackle.

This comical image is strengthened by the way they look. I cannot help but think of them as animated Toby jugs. They are fat and round, with pleasant faces and golden scales. They are almost in the goldfish class, except that they are not domesticated in any way, like the goldfish we usually find in garden ponds and glass bowls.

I rather like Dick Walker's comment about Crucians in his book *Stillwater Angling* (David and Charles). Dick says: 'A 2½lb roach looks a big fish, but a 2½lb Crucian is only a jolly, chubby little carp on which you've played a practical joke by catching him; and when you put him back, he scampers off full of beans. Like the Water Vole and the Little Owl, he attempts, but can never achieve, dignity'.

A lot of the big 'Crucians' we see reported in the angling press are, in fact, small common carp, so a word or two about identifying one from the other will not be amiss.

The colouring of Crucians and commons does not vary a great deal from water to water, but, if anything, the Crucian is slightly more 'brassy' along its flanks than the common carp. A Crucian is much more rotund in appearance than the common; its dorsal fin is convex, unlike the dorsal of a common which is concave; and the tail is much less forked than the common's. The most obvious difference between the two is the absence of barbules in the Crucian. Hybrids of the two do occur, but I do not believe they are as common as is popularly supposed. The identifying characteristics of a Crucian×Common hybrid are: barbules are usually present, but smaller than those found on the true common, and sometimes there are only two instead of four. It has 21 to 23 dorsal rays and 8 or 9 anal rays. The scale count along the lateral line is 35 to 38.

Big Crucians are not caught regularly, and I think of them as big when they weigh 2lb or more. A 3lb Crucian is an excellent specimen, and anything over 3lb is indeed a rare fish. When they reach 2lb they lose a lot of their yo-yo fight and really begin to bore off along the bottom, albeit for short distances. I think if more anglers had caught big Crucians they would soon forget their comical, easy image and fish for them with more respect and seriousness.

I cannot make up my mind whether big Crucians are more difficult to catch than we give them credit for, or the lack of press reports of big Crucians is due to their lack of popularity. I have to admit that half of the big Crucians I have caught have fallen to a bait meant for another species. The other half have been caught by design, but I can never fish for them continuously throughout a summer season; my interest soon switches to another species. But this does not mean that I do not enjoy catching Crucians when they are holding my interest.

They are shoal fish and the habits of smaller Crucian carp seldom vary. Week after week, you can fish the same swim and catch a similar bag of Crucians on each visit. Every time they will fall to the same method and bait at the same times, and rarely bite with either more or less ferocity or feebleness.

Big Crucians are like a different species. Very often you can fish a water for years and not even know Crucians are present. Then, one day, you will pull in a fish that fights differently to anything you have hooked on that water before, and it turns out to be a big Crucian. You realise straight away that these rotund fish must have been in the water for a long time, for you know that no recent stockings have taken place, and the fish is too big to have been there only a short time.

Big Crucians take angler's baits at irregular intervals; the cycle greatly varying from a few months to several seasons. You can have a really successful season on a lake and then two or three seasons when you will think that all the Crucians have passed away, for not one will come to your net. Why this should be so I have no idea, but a fact it is nonetheless. I am sure the fish are still present, even in the same swims where you have caught them before, but for some unknown reason they refuse to accept an angler's bait.

Crucians are found in all kinds and all sizes of stillwater, from the tiniest farm ponds to large gravel pits. Big Crucians are invariably found in the bigger waters, and are, indeed, a valuable asset to a big water. It is equally true that they are usually a liability in small waters, for they over-populate and become stunted in an incredibly short time, and thus deplete the natural larders with the inevitable result of curtailing the growth of other species. I have seen more small waters ruined through the introduction of Crucian carp than for any other reason. A one-acre pool I used to fish quite regularly some years ago produced big rudd, roach and tench. Then the club introduced a number of Crucians (more than the water could support anyway) and only three seasons later it was not fit to fish unless you enjoyed catching only a netful of small Crucians.

There is a distinct similarity between the behaviour of bream and Crucian carp in the way they patrol pre-determined beats and roll at the surface. But, unlike bream, Crucian beats are often no more than a rod's length from the bank and cover much shorter distances. Crucian beats are invariably in the vicinity of weed, and they particularly favour lilies. Wherever you find lilies in a Crucian water you should begin to search for the beats at the edge of the pads.

109

They seem to favour three- to six-feet depths, but this may be because lilies are also more likely to grow in this depth. They are warm weather fish, too, only rarely being taken after late September or early October. The shallow water is more favourable to summer fish.

Take the weather into account when choosing a swim. A water temperature between 60–70°F. is preferable, the exact temperature not being too important providing it is rising or steady. The side of the lake which the sun strikes first in the morning is often the best bet, and the opposite side in the evening; other swim conditions being equal of course.

Unlike some other species, Crucians do not seem to mind the surface being flat calm, and will feed quite willingly when there is less than a breath of wind to freshen the water. Therefore, when choosing a Crucian swim I am more concerned with depth of water, its temperature, and location of weeds, than I am the direction of wind, or lack of it.

Their rolling at the surface is often a dead give-away of their feeding patrol, so some time spent watching the water in the close season is time well spent. Many times, however, they roll beneath the surface, so a watchful eye for the brassy flash of a bronzed flank should be trained below the surface.

They bubble too, much the same as tench, but not quite with the same profusion. Crucian bubbles burst at the surface in small pockets rather than in large clumps. It is, though, difficult to distinguish between two or three tench pottering around on the bottom and half a dozen Crucians feeding in earnest.

Mudclouds caused by Crucians are not unknown, but are quite rare compared to how often bream cloud the water. So it is reasonable to assume that any mudclouds you see are more likely the result of rooting bream (skimmers) than Crucians. It is always worth investigating just the same. It is the only sure way to find out.

Most Crucian swims are within an easy float cast from the bank, and mainly it is with float tackle we fish for them. This is not to say that legering for Crucians should be discounted completely, but the very sensitivity of the way Crucians feed demands the most sensitive of tackle. Light link-legers or delicate paternoster rigs can and do catch Crucians, but these fish need to be feeding with none of their natural tentativeness for leger rigs to be consistently successful.

A free-line rig is thought by some anglers to be the most sensitive of all legering methods, but this is a fallacy (see chapter on tackle, page 7) and a short link-leger stopped close to the hook, or a short-tail paternoster is more likely to achieve results. The indicator should be light and only two or three inches of free line should be allowed. Strikes should be made at the merest twitch.

But where float tackle can be used, as it can in 90 per cent or more of Crucian swims, so it should be, so I propose to concentrate this section on Crucian tackle to float fishing.

You need look no further than a match rod for Crucian fishing. One of 12ft to 13ft is ideal, and the tip action of these rods can be useful when the Crucians are feeding even more delicately than usual, and you need to strike fast and sure at the merest twitch of the float.

A fixed-spool or centre-pin reel can be chosen, for it is extremely rarely you will need to cast more than two or three rod's length. So if you have an affection for centre-pin reel fishing, then go ahead and use one.

Lines for big Crucians should not be too light. In open water you can get away with a 2lb line, and let the fish have its own way for a while, pulling it to the net when it has used up most of its initial energy. But a 3lb line is much safer, even in open water, for a big Crucian, although lacking the sheer power of its bigger cousin, the common carp, can bore off in short bursts quite energetically. It is not very often, however, you find Crucians far from weed, especially tough lily stems, and a 4lb line is my choice on most occasions. In especially snaggy swims I have used a 5lb line, but I feel this is just that little bit too heavy and I never feel confident with it.

Floats should take as little shot as can be used, and a stick float which has the cane and balsa balanced to be almost self-cocking is my first choice. Delicate antenna-type floats are my second choice when there is wind causing a drift on the surface.

I use fine-wire, spade-end hooks, in sizes from 16 to 10. A 12 or 10 for flake, paste and worm, and 14 or 16 for casters, maggots, or small worms, or pieces of worm.

111

A good-sized Crucian carp.

I would not say that pre-baiting for Crucians is unnecessary, but it never worries me when I have to fish a Crucian swim that has not been baited. For one thing, groundbait will rarely draw Crucians away from their usual feeding route, and I have never found that Crucians become quite so preoccupied with natural food to the extent that most other species do.

They appear, most of the time, to be a very simple-minded fish that live uncomplicated lives in much the same drab way from day to day. They have a route, or routes, where they feed; they travel along these routes most, if not every day, feed at set intervals, and from time to time disappear completely, much to the puzzlement of the angler who has been catching them

112

regularly, only to re-appear again when memories of them have worn thin and they are least expected.

Groundbait on the day you fish is useful to the extent where it gives the Crucians a taste of your hookbait. One thing I can say quite adamantly; groundbait will not hold Crucians in your swim for very much longer than they would normally linger in that swim anyway. In fact, a single baiting a short while before you begin fishing is often enough to capture the fish's interest each time he passes that way. They do not stay long enough to overfeed, but will return often enough to feed on your groundbait during their non-stop commuting.

This ceaseless wandering from swim to swim is typical of the basic behaviour of Crucians. They suffer from St Vitus's Dance; they are never still. Even when feeding they are continually bobbing around, circling, pecking, shunting and making all manner of silly movements. They are excellent candidates for a fishy equivalent of John Cleese's Ministry of Silly Walks, perhaps re-named as Ministry of Silly Swimmers.

But these fidgety movements when feeding are not performed on the grand scale with elaborate, sweeping gestures. They are just that; fidgety, short, sharp and erratic. Our tackle set-up has to take this into account.

The float should be small and sensitive and take as little weight as can possibly be used, as should the line be only as heavy as is absolutely necessary. A single shot—no more than a dust-shot where it is possible to use one—should be placed on the line so that the float holds it a few inches off-bottom, and the float must be set so that the bait is just—and only just—touching the bottom.

The lift rig, as described in the chapter on tench (page 195), is also a useful method where you have to use more weight to reach the swim, or there is more drift than an off-bottom shot will cope with. It is not as efficient for Crucians, however, as the off-bottom shot method.

The biggest problem when Crucian fishing is knowing when to strike. Getting bites and seeing them is, relatively speaking, easy, compared to judging when the fish have actually got the bait in their mouths. It would be simpler if Crucian bites all took a similar form; then we could, after some experience, calculate

113

the best time to hit them. But big Crucian bites take many forms, from short, sharp dips; two or three inch trips of the float along the top without dipping or rising; the float describing small circles; the float rising and/or falling flat, to straightforward dips under the surface.

The rule of thumb I follow is to strike at all dips under the surface and any rises and falling flat of the float. When the float is circling or taking short trips along the top, or making minute dips without going under, I count to five and then strike. I cannot tell you why I count to five; it is not my lucky number, nor is it the result of an intelligent guess, but it works for me more often than counting to any other number, which, I suppose, is as good a reason as any.

Crucians do bite more boldly at night, but there are some waters where they never seem to feed at all at night, or they move to a route which is never fished. On waters where they do feed in darkness it is always a good idea to have a go for them then. They stay in a baited swim for longer periods and feed with less of the irrationality in which they indulge in the daytime.

In this instance you can use a float with a betalite tip which, of course, is heavier than the float you would normally use in daylight, and still get enough strikeable bites to make it interesting. I dislike using lights at night, but for Crucian fishing I make an exception, for I much prefer to stick to as light a float as possible and use a shielded torch to illuminate it.

The secret, if you can call it such, of using a torch on a float, is not to cast and manoeuvre the torch beam to shine on the float, but to set the torch beam to shine where you want to cast and leave it there. If you cast in the wrong spot, then you would do exactly the same as you would if you cast into the wrong spot in daylight: pull in and cast again. The beam should be set so that it skims the surface of the lake without shining into it, but you should have some thought for any anglers who are fishing on the opposite bank and avoid shining towards them. I know from experience that there is very little more annoying than a light shining in your eyes all night.

If you shine the beam into the water at a downward angle, to strike where the float is lying, this would avoid the problem of annoying other anglers, but it may not be very favourable to the fish. Experienced anglers have said that a light does not upset fish, and can, in fact, attract them. Perhaps it may attract some species and not others. I do know that fishing without lights shining into the water still catches fish; all species.

What I know about big Crucians is, to say the least, limited. I do not think that any angler can claim to know them well. This may be because there are few, if any, Crucian carp specialists. It is a pity really, but I cannot say I am surprised.

Dace

Of all the fish in which coarse fishermen take an interest the dace is the smallest. The largest dace ever taken on rod and line weighed 1lb 4oz 4drm, but one of 10oz is an excellent fish, and a 1lb dace can be classed as truly exceptional.

Dace of more than 1lb are very rare indeed, although you may hear of several being caught from time to time. Unless, however, you see the fish, or a detailed photograph, you can almost take it for granted that 'dace' of this weight are really small chub. The reason for this is the fact that inexperienced fishermen find it difficult to tell the difference between a small chub and a big dace, and fishermen being what they are, if a choice has to be made between a notable catch and an insignificant one there is, as the man on the television says, 'no contest'.

An angler who has caught a number of chub and dace should not have any difficulty in telling the difference, for a single glance is enough to earmark the fish for what it is. The dace has a more silvery appearance, the scales are smaller, the shape of the head is different, and the size and shape of the mouth are nothing like a chub's. If a single glance still leaves room for doubt, then look closely at the anal fin. The outer edge of the anal fin of the dace is concave, a chub's is convex.

Because dace are our smallest sporting species there is no reason for rating them as the least interesting. This is far from the truth, for a specimen dace needs as much thought and effort to capture it as any big fish, no less than pike and carp which are our largest coarse species.

116

Rivers that hold dace range from the smallest streams to waterways like the mighty Severn. Some stillwaters hold them too, but these are the exceptions rather than the rule. The interesting thing about these small fish is that it is usually the lesser known, small streams, that produce the biggest dace. My two best dace of 1lb and 1lb 1oz came from the Dane, a small river in Cheshire. I have never, in all the years I have fished it, seen anything approaching this weight come from the Severn. But the Severn does grow specimen fish of other species.

Big dace seem to prefer rivers which have plenty of character and it is usually our smallest rivers which are the most over-grown and twist and turn their way through the countryside. It is only in the upper reaches of our larger rivers where one can find the wild features and variety of swims that give a river a character of its own.

I have often wondered why a lot of specimen dace come from small rivers; why it should be that the middle and lower reaches of a large river, where the course is very canalised, very rarely produce them. Perhaps it is that fact; the lack of character, that has a lot to do with it. It is certainly true that dace prefer a variety of swims, each one differing in pace of current and depth of water, their tastes changing as they grow larger. Maybe it is because they cannot find the variety of swims they seem to need that they only rarely grow to specimen size on featureless waters.

Small dace up to 4oz or so can be found in vast shoals, and more often than not you will see these shoals of darting, flashing silver fish in fast water. They especially like the spot where a deep, slow glide meets a rise in the river bed; where the current suddenly surges forward and the smooth surface becomes broken as it tumbles over the ridges and weed in this shallower water.

Sometimes, but not always, one or two large dace may be sharing a fast-water swim with a shoal of small ones. But if you catch one from such a swim you can regard yourself as extremely fortunate, for very little in the way of bait gets past these agile youngsters once it hits the surface. Whenever I have seen a big shoal of small dace that held a couple of big ones, these two have always been at the tail-end of the shoal.

It may have been coincidence, but the times I have seen a shoal of small dace with bigger dace backing them up, there has always been just two big dace. One could be forgiven for thinking they were the parents keeping an eye on their offspring, or two older fish acting as security guards. I can offer no rational explanation, but it is a fact that two big dace often accompany a shoal of smaller ones, usually in the rear.

Apart from the odd big dace that prefer the company of a shoal of small ones, as dace grow bigger, exceeding about 6oz in weight, their choice of swim changes. They begin to move out of the really fast water and take up residence in the deeper, slower areas of a river. Dace up to 10oz or so still retain their strong shoaling instinct and can be taken in number from those gentle, slow glides that are so conducive to trotting with float tackle.

Big dace of more than 10oz in weight, while not entirely losing their shoaling instinct do, generally, break away from the main shoal and form small groups of up to a dozen or so fish. These tight-knit little communities seem to search out the comparatively slack water found under a cut-away bank, or even deep holes where the current is practically non-existent.

I have noticed, however, how often I have taken one or two big dace of 8oz or more when I have been chub fishing. Quite unexpectedly, after catching a few chub around the 3lb mark, I have had another cast and hooked a fish which, when playing it to the net, I have thought was a small chub. Then it has become apparent when the fish was netted and brought to hand for unhooking, that it was a large dace. This has happened so many times when I have been chub fishing I am convinced it is not an unusual feature of a dace's habits when it exceeds a certain size. Perhaps when they grow to a specific weight and begin to lead an almost solitary existence, having left the shoal of lesser fish and fed alone for a period, they come across a shoal of chub and, not having entirely lost the shoaling urge and by now missing the company of other fish, decide to join the chub which are more in line with the weight the dace has now attained.

I am rather more inclined to think though, that it is simply a case of the dace changing their choice of swim and feeding habits to the same preference as chub. We probably catch a big dace or two when chub fishing simply because we are fishing a swim that both species are partial to and both species happen to be feeding at that time. The only trouble with this side of the dace's character is the difficulty of selectively taking big dace from a swim they share with chub. Anything you can present to the dace to attract them, on whatever tackle, will certainly not deter the chub from having a go. Indeed, the dace are greatly outnumbered and, if anything, are considerably more wary than the chub anyway.

The only way you will consistently take these big dace from amongst a shoal of chub is to be able to see them through the surface, enabling you to drop a bait right under their noses, so that the chub do not get a chance to indulge first. Even then you are on a sticky wicket, for it is not as easy as it may seem. You must have some cover from which to cast, or the shoal, chub and dace alike, will take fright and be off in double-quick time.

Dace, like any other fish, however, should be sought according to the merits of the particular water that holds them. There are rivers which are not capable of growing big dace, and no matter which swims you choose to fish you will never take big dace from them. There are other rivers which do grow big dace, but only in isolated areas, usually the upper reaches, where you can apply what I have suggested earlier, and seek out the big ones. Yet again, there are rivers where it is more difficult to catch small dace than big ones. The environment is so ideal for growing quality dace the average weight could be 7oz or more. On such a river it will not matter greatly if you choose to fish the fast water for you will still catch big dace there; big that is, when compared to the average size of dace from most other rivers. You can still be selective on rivers such as this though, for the slow-flowing, cut-away banks and deep holes will probably hold even bigger dace, but instead of expecting to catch 8oz to 10oz fish, which are specimens in normal circumstances, you could catch those 12oz to 1lb dace which are the real specimens for that particular, exceptional piece of river. But that is what specimen hunting for any species is all about. Fish which are exceptionally big for one water will be only mediocre for another. It is up to you to recognise the degree of achievement wherever you are fishing.

Dace like bright sunshine; at least the normal run of dace do.

Where other fish will seek out the shaded spots, under thick weed and in the shadow of bankside foliage, dace will feed quite happily in the open swims with the sun highlighting their every movement, when their silver bodies flash as they twist and turn in the current, intercepting food at all levels in the water. Big dace, however, behave more in accord with how we expect fish to behave when the light is bright and their movements become obvious to all and sundry, both human and fishy predator alike.

Trotting the stream is the most popular and enjoyable method of fishing for dace, and in most instances is the most effective. The swims that dace choose to inhabit are usually tailor-made for them. Those long, slow glides for instance, where you can comfortably allow the float to ride down with the current for thirty yards or more.

Trotting is one of the most difficult and demanding arts in angling for the novice to master. The tackle, from float to hook, must be perfectly balanced. If it is not, then either the bait will not be presented to the fish in a natural manner, or a taking fish will not register a bite on the float. Even when the tackle has been assembled correctly it cannot be left, as it can on stillwater, to fish for itself. When the float trots down with the current the line must be frequently mended, which is a term given to the operation of flicking the bowing line off the water to always keep it riding behind the float and as straight as possible. Line should also be allowed to pull off the reel, whether it be a fixed-spool or centre-pin, as smoothly and easily as the current dictates. You should also have a clear mental picture of the bed of the river, so you know when you can let the float have its head, or when to hold back, allowing the baited hook to rise and ride over an obstacle. Holding back is a good idea too, when the fish, or some of them, are feeding in mid-water.

You can, of course, fish blind, initially, setting the fishing depth at an intelligent guess and adjusting it as you paint your mental picture on each trot through the swim. The other way is carefully to plumb the depth at strategic points from the head to the tail of the swim and then set the float at the most effective depth to deal with all or most of the variations. I am not sure which is the best method, or indeed, if there is a best method. On the one hand, a deal of fishing time is lost with the trial and error method, and only after a great many trots through the swim will you be fishing with utmost effect; on the other hand, plumbing the swim means disturbing the swim, especially on a small river. It is a case of taking each swim as you find it and using the method that best suits that swim.

I like to use a rod of at least 12ft long when I am trotting the stream, for any species that is, and one of 13ft is even better when fishing those wide stretches of river where the extra length will not be a hindrance in confined swims. One of the popular match rods is ideal for the purpose, both in lightness and action.

On a narrow river a centre-pin reel takes some beating. A good quality centre-pin that revolves easily from the slightest pull of the line makes trotting an even greater pleasure. It is simplicity itself to touch the drum with a finger-tip to control the tackle, and you can brake it instantly when you need to strike. With a fixed-spool reel the operation is a little more difficult, and line does not peel off the spool anywhere near as smoothly. But a fixed-spool reel comes into its own in distant swims where casting with a centre-pin takes a great deal of practice to master. Finally, a fixed-spool also has an advantage on the retrieve when the float has been allowed to trot a long way downstream.

It is a case of 'you pays your money and takes your choice' or, better still, save up and buy one of each and use the one most suitable for each swim you fish. You may, however, find that you are using the centre-pin almost exclusively for trotting once you have come to terms with casting with it.

I usually use a reel line of 2½lb and a hook length of 2lb. You will need hooks from size 20 to 12 depending on the bait you are using, and the response of the dace in the particular swim you are fishing on the day. Size 18 or 20 are handy for single maggot and caster fishing, and size 12 are useful for the bigger dace which usually prefer bread or a small worm.

For very fast, ruffled-surface swims, a cork-bodied, well-shotted float will do the job. But for most dace swims the simple 'stick' float is one of the best. The stick float is made from a stem of cane, or wire, topped with an inch or two of balsa. You can make your own quite easily and have a selection to cover all manner of swims. For faster swims you would use more balsa than you would for slower swims for, obviously, you do not need as many shot to keep the bait down where the current is on the slow side, and the more balsa you use the more buoyancy the float will have, therefore needing more shot to cock it properly.

Legering for dace, especially the big ones, should not be disregarded, for the twilight period and an hour or so into darkness is one of the best times to catch a specimen dace. My dace fishing these days takes in the two methods. I will fish through the day with float tackle, thoroughly enjoying trotting the stream and catching dace from 4oz to 7oz or so, and then I will change to leger tackle as soon as it becomes too dark to see the float. A typical day's dace fishing, for me, goes something like this:

I arrive at the water about 8.30 a.m. The sun is bright and there is no breeze to ripple the surface of the small river I have chosen to fish. I have enjoyed a lie in bed this morning, for I know the dace will feed, off and on, throughout the day in spite of, or because of, the bright sunshine.

I choose a swim which is about twenty-five yards long, of medium pace until it reaches the spot where the bottom shelves up and the water rushes over at a greater speed. The water under the far bank, some six or seven yards away, is five feet deep, and the bottom slopes up to my own bank over a sandy bed. My own bank is open, but lining the far bank are a few hawthorn bushes, two alders, and at the tail-end of the swim, a huge, ancient, crack willow tree that threatens to tumble across the river it leans over so alarmingly.

Although my own bank lacks any foliage to give me cover from the fish, I am not too worried, for the bank rises steeply behind me, so my movements will not be exaggerated against the clear blue sky. Even so, I position my fold-up chair a few yards upstream of the head of the swim and tackle up well away from the river. Whilst I was positioning my chair I threw half a dozen floating casters into the swim and watched them glide slowly down the oily surface, expecting one or two to be taken at any time. But they reached the rise in the river bed, beneath a branch of the crack willow, before just one was sucked into a hungry mouth.

I am not unduly surprised to find the dace are in the fast water at the tail of the swim. Invariably they lie in shallow, well-oxygenated water when the weather is hot and sultry. I would have to try to tempt them upstream a bit into the slower, deeper water, if I am going to make a good netful. I could catch a few from the shallows of course, but I would have to wait quite a while after hooking each fish because of the disturbance a hooked fish would create when struggling to shed the hook. The subtle use of loose feed and groundbait should draw them up sufficiently.

I go back to my chair, carrying rod, landing net and keepnet, and my rucksack which contains a baitbox of maggots and a small box of redworms. I also have a fresh, thin-sliced loaf, which I find better than solid loaves for pinching pieces off to bait small hooks; a 4-pint bait bucket for mixing groundbait; a flask of coffee and a pack of sandwiches. Finally, of course, my tackle box.

I cautiously approach my fishing position and lay out the items around me, everything within easy reach of my chair so that I can fish with a fluid motion with movements restricted to a minimum. I spread my keepnet down the sandy slope to the right, where it will not interfere with the landing of fish, and take care to stake it out at the bottom so that the net will not collapse and fish will be in sufficiently deep water to stop them splashing.

The next job is to mix about 8oz of groundbait, which is plenty to be going on with. I put the water in the bucket first, which is opposite to my usual way of mixing groundbait, and then slowly add the groundbait until the mixture is pretty solid and will take some time to break up on the bottom, which is the reason I am mixing it 'the wrong way round'.

My idea is to compress a tennis-ball-size piece of groundbait into a cup shape, fill the cup with at least a dozen maggots and then close up the cup into a ball. This I drop into the head of the swim where it will slowly dissolve and break up from the wriggling of the maggots and allow them to trickle slowly through the swim along the bottom. A bait dropper, which is a mechanical box for releasing loose feed along the bed of the river, would not do the same job, for such a device releases the feed in one fell swoop, whereas my slowly dissolving groundbait ball frees the maggots steadily over a period of time. This is important to achieve my objective, which is to lay a path of loose feed down the swim which the dace will follow out of the shallow water into the deeper water where I prefer and hope to catch them. It is true that a ball of mud would do a similar job, with less risk of overfeeding, but the use of groundbait is an integral part of my plan, which is to give the big dace at least a smell of bread, if not taste, for the time when darkness falls and I change to leger tactics and flake or crust as hookbait.

I reckon a ball of feed every twenty minutes, plus a dozen or so maggots thrown in loose every other cast, ought to keep them interested without unduly over-feeding them. The amounts I have specified will vary from swim to swim according to the fish population in each swim, and how well or not they are feeding on the particular day you fish.

I bait my hook with a single maggot and then cast towards the far bank with more power than is really necessary, but brake the tackle by dropping a finger onto the lip of the spool. This braking action causes the tackle to fall onto the surface in a straight line and so ensures that there are no tangles. If I had cast with only just enough power to reach the distance required, the tackle would have landed in a heap and most likely would have stopped that way as it trotted down the swim.

The cast is good and I draw back a few inches to avoid the straggly branch of the hawthorn and so allow the float a clear run all the way through the swim. Fortunately, the float does not complete its run, for a dace has seized the maggot after only three yards. I strike and hook the fish, swing the rod over towards my own bank and keep the tip low to stop the fish from splashing at the surface. The fish—I know it is a dace now because of the distinct jagging on the rod—gives a spirited fight but soon finds itself being drawn into my landing net. It looks about 6oz. Not a bad start.

Two casts later I catch another dace from the same spot, but in the next few casts I take a couple of fish within seconds of the hook reaching the bottom. More casts and more fish later, with a groundbait/maggot ball and the occasional handful of loose feed still going into the river, the dace I am catching are tending to come further and further away, no doubt because of the inevitable disturbance a few of the fish made when I hooked them, and the loose feed which is reaching further downstream.

This is the usual pattern of events when dace trotting, and I find it best to lay the rod down for ten or fifteen minutes while I have a sandwich and a cup of coffee and do nothing more than feed the swim. This I now do, and when I begin fishing again I find that the dace have regained confidence and have begun once more to follow the loose feed towards its source.

This pattern, taking fish at increasing distances and then encouraging them to move up river again, continues throughout the day. A couple of the fish are around the 8oz or 9oz mark, but no sign of the 12oz-plus dace that move into the swim on occasion. But darkness is moving in pretty fast now and I know that the bigger dace will soon be rooting in the hollows of the far bank.

I strip the float tackle off my line and tackle up with a two swan-shot link-leger and a size 10 hook tied direct to the 2lb reel line. Onto the hook I pinch a halfpenny-size piece of flake and cast into the black hole between two branches on the far bank. The rod is placed in the rod-rest directly in front of me and I hold the butt in my right hand. The middle finger of my left hand is curled around a loop of line pulled from between butt-ring and reel. If I preferred, I could have changed the rod and used a swing-tip or quiver-tip as a bite indicator, but no mechanical device is as effective and efficient as my sense of touch, so there is no point, is there? (See pages 12–15.)

My first bite is a savage pull that digs the line into my finger as the fish hooks itself. I bully it out of the dark hole as quickly as I can, trying to keep the swim as undisturbed as possible. The dace is a satisfying 9oz.

My next cast falls short by about twelve inches, but I leave it there.'just in case'. I do not get a bite in the next ten minutes however, which is as I expected, for the bigger dace hug the far bank and can rarely be tempted out. I recast a fresh bait and this time it lands accurately. Five minutes later the line trembles on my finger and I steel myself ready to strike. But nothing else happens and I am telling myself I should pull in because my bait is gone, when the tremble starts again, then again, and I respond with a quick flick of the rod-tip which connects with a good dace of 11oz. I take two more dace of around the same weight in the next hour and then call it a day.

I know I could have taken more fish if I had stayed a while longer, but I also know that the dace will still be there, in that swim, for a long time to come and I will have many more chances to catch them. Short of a raging flood that could change the nature of the swim, dace very rarely move from one swim to another.

Eels

The eel is a very intriguing fish. Unlike other coarse fish, it is catadromous, leaving freshwater to spawn in the sea. It is the Sargasso Sea where they spawn, and when the tiny leptocephalus are hatched they are carried across the Atlantic by the Gulf Stream. When they arrive at the European continental shelf they change form, or metamorphose, to elvers, and swim up the nearest rivers, particularly those on the west coast. This has only been known since as recently as 1920, but it is their life in freshwater of which we know so little. We do know that they feed in our lakes and rivers for several years, until the urge to spawn dominates their instincts and drives them down the rivers and back to the sea.

There are very few waters in Britain that do not contain eels, including those which do not have any apparent connection with rivers by way of feeder and outlet streams. How the elvers find their way into these enclosed waters is still unknown, but theories range from the probability of their following an underground route that emerges as a spring through the bottom of a lake, to the possibility of them being able to navigate overland.

There are so few, if any, authenticated instances of elvers being discovered wriggling through meadows or any other terrain it is doubtful whether their amphibious activities are based on fact. It is true, however, that an eel can live for an incredibly long time out of water, and that an eel which is carried away from the edge of a lake, even three hundred yards or more, will always turn and wriggle overland towards the lake.

127

I have experimented with a freshly caught eel several times and it is uncanny how they turn immediately towards the water and slither through the grass with the same ease and ability as a terrestrial snake. I would not like to say with any conviction whether or not it is part of the eel's natural behaviour to travel overland to reach and depart from land-locked waters.

Land-locked waters also form the basis of a theory regarding really big eels. It is said in some circles that giant eels are found in lakes which have no connection with rivers. The lake may have a tiny stream running into it which elvers can negotiate with ease, but which is too small to allow mature eels to escape. Larger streams might be blocked by grids or a curtain of wire mesh, the openings of which are large enough to allow elvers to enter, but too small to allow a grown eel to leave.

This is known as the 'prison' theory, and it assumes that an imprisoned eel will continue to feed and grow in that water for many years after it has reached maturity. This may be so, but 'prison' waters are by no means the exclusive territory of big eels. There are many waters that contain big specimens which do have access to rivers.

The growth rate of eels must to a large extent depend, as it does with all living creatures, on the availability and quality of food, and the competition for that food. In waters where you are continually being pestered by small eels (bootlaces) you very rarely hear of large eels of 3lb and over being caught. The opposite is true too; where eels of 2½lb to 3lb are common, you are rarely bothered by bootlaces.

I think we can safely assume that a rich 'escapable' water, where there is little competition, will grow bigger eels than a poor 'prison' water where competition is great. The ideal of course, assuming there is some significance to the 'prison' theory, is a 'prison' water rich in quality food and with very little competition for that food. But it is also true that there is a great variation in the growth rate of eels in the same water. The reason for this may not have any connection with food quality and quantity in that water, but may be linked with the elver's time of arrival and the type and quantity of food it consumed during its journey. The early years of any creature's life, whether it fed richly or poorly, almost inevitably has an influence on its progress in later years. An undernourished young creature is usually a poor specimen throughout its life.

To what size it is possible for eels to grow in first-class conditions has always been a great debating point, and a controversial one too. The record now stands at 11lb, but there are tales of 20lb and even 30lb specimens on record, but not authenticated. That they do grow bigger than 11lb there is no doubt, but I cannot believe they are capable of even approaching 20lb.

Very big eels are not often caught, mainly because they are not a popular species, and usually when one is hooked accidentally it makes short work of the inadequate tackle. If pike fishing were more of a summer occupation then I believe we would see more giant eels caught, for pike tackle, with its use of a wire-trace, is quite capable of dealing with a big eel. As it is, pike fishing is traditionally a winter pursuit, and eels very rarely feed in winter conditions.

Only a comparative handful of dedicated anglers, most of them belonging to the National Anguilla Club, make a determined and prolonged effort to contact giant eels. The eel's lack of popularity is not due to it being an easy opponent or a poor fighter, for the opposite is true. It is because, to most people, the eel is distasteful, a reptilian beast that is slimy and vicious and conjures up horrific thoughts. Very small eels do not help their image either. In waters where they are prolific they make a catastrophic mess of end-tackle and a decided nuisance of themselves. They breed loathing of them as a species at a very early age; a loathing I am sure, that remains in anglers' minds for all time.

If, however, anglers made a conscious effort to catch a big eel, I am sure they would look at them in an entirely different light. I have found that the more big eels I catch, the more affection and respect for them I develop. Familiarity gradually kills their distasteful image and teaches one that they can be as much fun and as challenging to seek as any other species.

Many times I have heard anglers say something like, 'There I was playing this fish, when all of a sudden I saw it was a bloody great eel. I pulled for a break. I didn't fancy unhooking that!'

I suppose this attitude is understandable in a way; the poor angler was expecting to see a friendly tench come to his net, when suddenly he was confronted with the lashing gyrations of an eel. It does not require a big eel to instil this feeling of horror; a 2-pounder is longer than a big tench.

Yet this same feeling of horror becomes the same sense of excitement to an angler who set his stall for eels, and is fully expecting that long, writhing body to appear at the surface. It is a different excitement to the one you feel when you land, say, a big carp. I suppose it is still tinged with a hint of fear, but an element of fear or horror is part of the pleasure.

How then do we find a water that holds big eels? There are only two reliable ways; one of them is to learn of them from other anglers or local people who know the history of the water, and the other is to fish each water you suspect could hold big eels for a reasonable period until your suspicions have been confirmed or denied. There are no other means, for all types and sizes of waters can hold eels and you can only find out to what size the eels grow by reliable information, or by catching a few.

Big eels are predatory, but do not rely entirely on a fish diet. Much depends on the water where the eel lives, and the abundance or otherwise of fish of suitable size for the eel to feed on. They are opportunist feeders and scavengers. If they are presented with a profusion of spawn at the appropriate time of year they will quite happily feed on spawn. Dead fish which have not yet begun to decompose are taken with relish, and if there is nothing more substantial readily available they are content to grub for crustacea, molluscs and larvae, and it is not unknown for them to eat vegetable matter. In the stomachs of eels gutted for research or for the pan have been found the remains of mice, birds, frogs and slugs.

Several years ago I was fishing at night for bream on a Shropshire mere and a friend, Mike Rushworth, was fishing for eels some two hundred yards further down the same bank. In the morning I went to see if Mike had caught anything and he lifted out a sack which disgorged three eels from 2lb to 2¼lb. As they writhed on the grass there was a loud belch and one of the eels spewed out the part-digested head and both legs of a young coot. The legs, complete with feet, and the head, minus

Graham Marsden holds a 5lb eel he took on lobworms from a Cheshire mere.

feathers, were intact, which suggested the bird had hardly been chewed, but swallowed whole. When you consider that such a small eel could gorge a relatively big bird like that it makes you

131

wonder what a big eel could do. Full-grown coots, ducks, and other water fowl should not be considered safe.

Generally though, the bigger the eel, the more their diet consists of fish, and it is with fish we have the best chance of catching them, especially on waters where there are smaller eels, for small fish of three to six inches are more selective than worms. Worms are, however, an excellent bait for eels, and big eels too, but they are not selective. A 1lb eel can take a big bunch of lobs just as easily as a 5-pounder can, but a small deadbait is more likely to select the better specimens. On waters where there are few, if any, small eels, then a bunch of lobs is as good as anything.

Choosing an eel swim is more of a hit and miss affair than it is for any other species. You cannot rely on observation alone, for eels, as a rule, do not roll or show at the surface. When I tackle an eel water I know nothing about I base my judgment on where I would choose to fish for roach or rudd. If I know an area is attractive to a small species than I know it will be attractive to eels too, and if there are any weedbeds or other snags in the area, then so much the better.

You can create an eel swim almost anywhere in a fishery by pre-baiting with fish guts, blood, worms, offal, etc. I have done so quite a few times, but I doubt whether I will do it again. The trouble is, a pre-baited eel swim seems to attract all the small eels in the water, and while no doubt it attracts big eels too, they have little or no chance to get to your bait before a small one. It is quite incredible how big a bait a small eel can take, and if it cannot consume it in one go, it nibbles away at it until it can. So a big bait will not be too selective.

Tackle for big eels should be strong; much stronger than the weight of the fish you expect to catch suggests. A big eel is a powerful fighter, though no more powerful than a tench, carp or barbel of comparable weight. What you have to contend with where eels are concerned, however, is their unique ability to wrap their tails around any convenient obstacle and become immovable, while at the same time striving to wind your line around the obstacle and so make their escape. The obstacle does not have to be a sturdy branch or root that trails into the water, a boulder or other solid object; it need only be several strands of tough weed. The well-known ploy of giving slack line to a weeded fish rarely succeeds with eels. The only answer is to employ brute force against brute strength, and for this you need very stout tackle.

You do not play an eel, giving or gaining line as the situation dictates, at least not without the risk of losing it. You use very strong tackle and give no quarter whatsoever. Once the hook is driven home you heave with all your strength and pump the fish straight to the bank and haul it right onto the grass—where the margins are suitable—or into a large landing net. The idea is not to give the eel even half a chance to whip his tail around anything; you turn him with that first mighty heave and then keep him coming in as straight a line as possible, and as quickly as possible, so preventing him from winding his body into a swimming posture.

In reasonably open water this line of attack works very well, but there are many instances where you must fish quite close to snags, even amongst them, to hook eels in the first place. This is when the fun starts and when you congratulate yourself for choosing stout gear. Many times the eel will already have his tail lashed around a snag while he munches your bait, and when you strike it is as though you have hooked the snag; solid and unmoving. Then the eel begins to shake his head and you realise what has really happened. Brute force, even to the extent of handlining, with a leather glove on for protection, is your only chance of winning this test of strength.

I favour an 11ft rod of 2lb test-curve and a line of no less than 12lb b.s. I do, though, use a 2¾lb test-curve rod and a 15lb line when fishing in especially snaggy waters. A fixed-spool reel with the clutch mechanism locked tight, or a multiplying reel are best. Many eel anglers swear that wire traces are essential, as necessary as they undoubtedly are for pike. I have mixed feelings on this issue, for there is something to be said for wire-traces and for traceless rigs.

There are times when eels can be extremely fussy and drop the bait before a run has developed. This happens most often when a wire-trace is employed. This is not due to the fact that the wire is thick and obvious, but to the stiffness and the resultant lack of natural 'feel' to the bait. Tying the hook direct to the reel line certainly produces more positive runs, but it means you are taking a chance on the eel's abrasive palate fraying and eventually severing the line. My answer is to compromise by employing a 25lb b.s. braided terylene leader. This is supple enough (more supple than 15lb nylon monofil in fact) not to discourage positive runs as is the case with wire, and so far I have not had the slightest misgivings about its strength and resistance to fraying.

To be fair to the 'wire addicts' however, I must point out that I use a leader for one eel only and then discard it, whether it shows signs of wear or not. My method is to have several leaders already made up with hook and swivel. At the end of my reel line I have a link swivel which makes it easy to change leaders very easily and quickly. When I catch an eel I simply unclip the link swivel and drop the eel into a sack with the hook and leader still attached, and then fit a new leader. At the end of the session I unhook the eels, release them or despatch them, and take the used leaders home and burn them after salvaging the swivels.

I use size 6, eyed hooks for worm fishing and size 2's for deadbaits. Whenever possible I fish a free-line rig, only using lead on the line when I cannot reach a distant swim without it. I have never float-fished for eels, but do not doubt that it is a very effective method, especially with betalite floats at night. In fact I know this will work, for I have taken eels to 5lb on a betalite float while fishing for other species. The only trouble is that I, and many other eel anglers, fish for eels in the coarse close season and suspended lines are not allowed in some River Authority areas. Check on this before you try it.

Roach and rudd from three to six inches long are good baits for eels, but if you want the best, then catch a few gudgeon. Eels love them. You need a baiting needle to fish them properly. You push the needle in at the root of the tail and draw it out through the mouth, attach the line to the hook and then draw it back until the bend of the hook is curled round the scissors of the mouth so only the point is visible.

I set the rod in two rests in the usual legering manner, using a Gardner 'Monkey Climber' type indicator and an Optonic bite alarm. I leave the bale-arm of the reel open when deadbait fishing, for eels usually run with the bait and you need to let them take a few yards of the line before striking to ensure the hook is fully in their mouths. I leave the bale-arm closed when worm fishing, and strike at the first indication.

This quick striking when worm fishing is still often met with a throat-hooked eel. I usually use three to five large lobworms, but this writhing mass is engulfed in double-quick time, even by small eels no more than 1lb in weight. I have struck at no more than a couple of half-inch twitch bites and still found the eel was throat-hooked. Only rarely does an eel run with worms, so be prepared for short, sharp bites, and plenty of yo-yo action as the indicator rises and falls. Total alertness, or an electric bite alarm, are essential when worm fishing to avoid deeply hooked eels.

There are times when eels will pick up a deadbait and then drop it, even when using a leader instead of a wire trace. I do not know what makes them do this, but it could be that they have felt the hook or are suspicious of something else. Perhaps it is merely a question of the finicky mood they are in. When this happens you can often induce a take by twitching the bait along the bottom. The moment you feel a pluck on your finger, release the line and wait for the run. If no run develops, then begin, but gently, to twitch the bait again. If the eel is still felt when you pull the line, then strike, for the odds are that the eel is gorging the bait on the spot.

There are so many ways advocated for dealing with eels once you have landed them it is no wonder the beginner is confused as to which is best. These methods range from the crude— putting your foot on them (which is ineffective)—to the spiritual: gouging the shape of a crucifix in the earth and laying the eel on its back inside the upright. This method does work, but not for religious reasons; it is equally effective if you dig a simple furrow with no cross-piece.

I simply grip the eel behind the head, using a cloth, and have very little trouble.

Perch

There are very few perch specialists in the country, which is unusual, for we have anglers who specialise in at least one of all other species. I have often wondered why this should be so, for a big perch is a fine fish which anyone should be proud to catch.

The availability of big perch has decreased through disease in the last few years, but it is too easy to blame this for the absence of perch hunters. Even before the decimation of perch there were only a few perch catchers of any note. The daddy of them all was Dick Walker, who sorted them out in Arlesey lake in the early 'fifties. Another was Alan Southern who also made some fabulous catches of big perch from a Cheshire lake in the late 'sixties. Apart from those two stalwarts I can think of no-one who has successfully made a persistent effort to catch big perch. There are, however, a number of anglers, myself included, who have occasionally made some fine catches of perch of more than 2lb each in weight. But there is a difference in occasionally fishing for big perch and specialising in them for a prolonged period. For one thing, the specialist has more blanks! But one can learn from blank days, even if it is only acquiring a knowledge of what not to do.

So why are there so few, if any, perch specialists?

We should ask ourselves first why we specialise in any species, and the obvious answer is that the particular species we fish for more than any other has a special attraction for us. The fish most anglers favour is the roach and the special attraction here is their wide availability, and the fact that a big roach is a prize that everyone appreciates. At the other end of the scale, size-wise, are carp, and the special attraction here is the powerful fight that ensues when one is hooked. There are other reasons, of course, just as there are reasons for specialising in any species. Except perch.

Perch are beautiful fish, so the reason for their lack of popularity cannot be ugliness. Even eels have their devout followers and nothing puts people off more than does a reptilian likeness. Perch are not hard fighters, but neither are bream, and they are a popular species. I can only think there is a psychological reason behind it all, in that perch were probably the first fish that most anglers caught as boys. As a result they are probably associated, at least in small sizes, with canes, bent pins and garden worms. Small ones are also regarded as nuisances when an angler has his stall set for the ever-popular roach.

For these reasons, perch are thought of as easy fish to catch, as they are when they are small, but the stigma follows through and remains in an angler's mind, albeit at the back, for a long long time. Who wants to specialise in an easy fish; a nuisance fish, that takes knotted worms on bent pins tied to cotton? Nobody, except those who have deliberately tried to catch big perch and have realised the folly of thinking that they are easy.

Make no mistake, perch are no different to any big fish as far as difficulty in catching them is concerned. In fact, I think less is known about the habits of big perch than any other fish; nobody has spent long enough in their pursuit and studied their behaviour. There is so little we know about big perch, and this is borne out by the fact that even accidental captures of them are far fewer than any other species.

I am, however, going to tell you how to catch them, or at least how I have caught a few in the past. But before I do, let me be the first to say that much of what I will be telling you is not the result of original thinking, but a mixture of what has been gleaned from other anglers, and my own experiences. From there you can use the information and no doubt enrich it from your own adventures with big perch.

The perch is a predator and, in the smaller sizes, hunts in packs like the African wild dogs. It is often called the freshwater tiger, not because of its behaviour, but because of the distinctive black stripes that cross its body from back to belly. It has two dorsal fins, the front one being large and spined, which it spreads out like a peacock's tail when alarmed or angry. You can see it do this when you unhook one; if you are unlucky you will also feel it! You should also beware of the sharp, cutting edge of the gill cover. The scales of the perch are rough to the touch and the ventral and anal fins are a brilliant orange colour, the tail a bright red, making it a unique fish which cannot be confused with any other. The record is 5lb 9oz.

Very small perch feed mainly on crustacea, but when it grows to more than ¾lb or so it becomes almost exclusively a fish eater, although this depends mainly on the availability of food fish of a takeable size. If a water is poor in food fish then the perch can be quite content, indeed has to be content, to scavenge for any small animals that are going. In this case, however, it is extremely unlikely that the perch will grow to an interesting size.

Once perch have grown out of the infant stage and show an interest in killing, including cannibalism, they can be likened to the African wild dog to an even greater degree. They pursue, chase and harass their prey relentlessly, and just as wild dogs rush in and sever the leg tendons of the victim to slow it down, so the perch dart in to nip repeatedly at the tail fin of the victim until it can no longer swim fast enough to escape.

Another of their ploys, and I have been lucky enough to see it in action, is to surround a shoal of fry and methodically decimate them. It is like a battle scene, with both perch and fry moving across the surface as one, as though in slow motion. Several of the perch, but never enough to leave a bolt hole for the victims, dash into the shoal and grab, or attempt to grab, a fry. Then others take their turn.

I had the advantage of seeing this performance from a high vantage point; the bough of a tree where I was bream spotting. On a near level with the water it looks like an isolated pocket of rain travelling across the surface. This, of course, is the fry showering through the surface in a futile attempt to escape the marauding perch.

I have seen this showering effect many times, and although suspecting perch or small pike to be the cause of the fry's

138

'The Sergeant': a 2lb perch.

distress, I have never before had occasion to witness this
enthralling spectacle from a suitable vantage point. Nor was this
high level view the only advantage; another was the crystal-clear
water, which is essential to perch for they hunt mainly by sight.
This is why it is extremely rare for big perch to be found in a
water which is well stocked with carp, for such waters are
always murky, if not downright muddy, from the constant
rooting of carp on the bottom.

The only exception to this rule that I know is the Cheshire

139

lake where Alan Southern caught his big perch. This water is large and shallow (which is normally another factor not associated with big perch) and holds a large head of both big and small carp as well as the several shoals of perch, of which some were exceptionally big. The only thing that sets this water apart from any other, which could account for big perch being found in a water otherwise totally unsuitable for them, is that at one time it was the site of salt excavations. It seems that perch thrive in a water with a high saline content; the Norfolk Broads, being so near to the sea, are another example.

It is also said that perch and carp are not compatible because the perch are very partial to carp spawn, which they feed ravenously on at the appropriate time of year. Here again, the Cheshire lake was the exception to the rule.

The larger a perch grows the more solitary it becomes; it changes from a wild dog to a panther. Instead of stalking prey in a pack and relying on sheer weight of numbers to break down a victim, it lies in ambush and strikes suddenly, consuming its prey without so much as a warning bite.

The perch is perfectly designed to attack by ambush. Its camouflage alone is ideally suited to its situation; the dark, vertical bars matching exactly the play of light that filters through a ripple on the surface. The wrist of the tail and the tail itself is small and lacks the power to chase and catch a victim over any distance. A tail like that is meant for short bursts of speed, such as a sudden strike from the cover of weed. I am not sure if the perch's sharp gill covers are an attacking weapon or a defensive weapon, but I do know that a 3lb perch can swallow another fish weighing as much as ½lb.

In summer the perch is a roamer and they roam wherever their food fish take them, which is mainly in the shallower areas of lakes where the water is warmer and richer in plant and animal life. Fry and small fish move around in big shoals of mixed species, not usually moving far away from the comparative safety of marginal weeds. The fact that these small fish gather in large shoals is, of course, ideal for the perch, for they have easier pickings when they can attack a mobile larder rather than isolated food items.

Perch can be more difficult to catch in summer than in

winter, for in the warm months they have little difficulty in satisfying their appetites, and the fact that they roam so much means they are that much harder to find. The temperature in the shallower areas of a lake is also more liable to fluctuation, and the food fish and perch alike react accordingly.

One of my favourite ways of catching perch in summer is to roam the margins of a lake in a boat. (The tackle and techniques can also be applied, with slight moderations, to roach.) I position the boat an easy cast from the margins and use a simple float rig. This is usually a piece of peacock quill attached to the line by a rubber at top and bottom. Onto the 5lb b.s. line I tie an eyed size 6 hook on which I impale a big lobworm. Directly under the float, I pinch a single swan-shot, which is sufficient to cock the float so that only an inch remains above surface. A big lobworm is heavy enough to travel ahead of the float when cast and if everything is balanced right, and you cast with a lobbing action, the worm will hit the surface first with the float following.

The idea is to cast right into the gaps between reed stalks, or in holes between the floating leaves of plants such as amphibious bistort. Ensure that both top and bottom rubbers are flush with the ends of the float, then there will be less likelihood of snagging when playing a fish, or when retrieving the tackle.

Bites usually come suddenly, for the perch takes the worm with the same speed of strike as it would use to attack a small fish. As soon as the float shoots under you should strike, for any delay means that the perch can wrap your line around the weed stalks. Only rarely will you miss fish by striking quickly, for the perch can and usually does, very easily engulf a big lobworm in one fell swoop.

If, however, you fail to get a take in the first few minutes, tighten up to the float and waggle the rod-tip. This will make the worm jiggle about in the water and the vibrations, and the sight of it, will help to attract perch to your bait. Once a perch has been taken in this way, wait no longer than about fifteen minutes, for very often it will be the only perch in that area.

Another method I use for catching perch in summer is to go rudd and roach snatching! Tackle up for catching small rudd and roach and also rig up another rod for perch, which for the time being you set to one side.

141

The idea is to work up the swim with cloud groundbait, and perhaps maggots too, to attract a big shoal of small rudd and/or roach. These small fish, completely pre-occupied with competing with each other for the loose feed will, we hope, attract a few big perch who hope to feed on the small fish. Of course, you have no need to continue fishing for the food fish once you have got a few for hookbait; you can quite easily accomplish what you are trying to do simply by sitting there with a basin of cloud groundbait. Catching the food fish while waiting for the perch to come along is just something to pass the time away; snatching little rudd and roach is better than catching nothing, I think.

You will know the perch have arrived when you see a spiny dorsal cleave through the surface, but if all you see is the fry scattering here, there and everywhere, then it could be a pike; probably a small jack. Still, it just may be a perch, so cast a bait-fish amidst the rumpus and see what happens.

I favour a paternoster rig for this kind of fishing, with a ¾oz bomb on the bottom and a piece of peacock quill on the surface. I set the split ring or swivel about six inches deep and use a hook length about nine inches long. I use a fairly heavy weight so that I can jiggle the bait without moving the tackle from where I have cast it. The hook is a single size 6, slid lightly through the top lip of the bait. After a few minutes, if no take results, then resume feeding the cloud groundbait around the float of your bait-fish rig. This may not attract the rudd back for a while, so soon after being marauded, but the sight of the cloud could attract the perch again now that they have associated the white cloud with a shoal of food fish.

What I have tried with some success is changing the single size 6 hook for two small trebles, tied in tandem about four inches apart. Then I have impaled a baitfish on each of the points, making a shoal of six hookbaits in all. When I first tried it I had fears that the two fish on the points of the treble adjacent to the one a perch went for, would stop the perch from getting the hook into its mouth. But it has not worked out like that in practise, for very often the perch has two or more of the baits in its mouth as well as the hook. Whether the perch deliberately went for more than one fish I do not know. It may be that the perch went for just one bait, but the fact that two others were inseparable from it caused the fish, like it or not, to engulf two or more.

Line of 4lb b.s. is usually ample for most perch fishing, but I like to use 6lb when there are pike around, for this gives me a better chance of landing them. Not that I want to catch a jack pike, but I do want to get my tackle back!

Lure fishing, with plug, spoon or spinner is better done from a boat, for a boat allows you to spin on a parallel line along the margins, which is where a lot of big perch are found during the summer months. This is especially so if there are bankside trees whose branches have sagged into the water, or whose roots have become bare and offer the perch good ambushing spots.

I have often heard anglers arguing whether it is best to use a fast or a slow retrieve when spinning for perch. They usually back up their arguments by relating the number of times they have taken perch when spinning at great speed, or when retrieving at a snail's pace, whichever the case may be.

In my view, you cannot go far wrong if you set out to imitate the actions of a small fish, which, when all is said and done, swim both fast and slow. After all, this is what a spinning lure is meant to represent. My retrieve, therefore, is a mixture of snail's pace and great speed, sometimes coming to a dead stop, and then suddenly whipping the rod-tip back to make the lure dart forwards and upwards in the water, and then letting it sink slowly to the bottom again. Sometimes I wind at speed for ten yards or more and then cover another ten yards winding just fast enough to stop the lure from snagging the bottom. It is a question of experimenting; finding out which action, if any in particular, is taking the most fish on that day, in that swim, and then retrieve accordingly.

I must say, however, that I am not very impressed with spinning for any species. I find it boring, and confess to only employing this method when all else fails. Apart from anything else, it is the least likely method to catch a big perch, and will more likely result in several jack pike, which you can well do without when your sights and your tackle are set to catch a goodly 'sergeant'.

I think it is worth mentioning that fly fishing with a sunken line and a bright lure also takes perch, though it is not, in my experience, selective for big ones. I have caught plenty of perch on fly, but only by accident when trout fishing. I am not, therefore, really qualified to say whether fly fishing would be a good method or not.

Dick Walker once took twenty-three perch from 2lb to 3lb from Hanningfield reservoir on a lure while fly fishing for trout. The lure on which he took most of the perch was one he had designed himself to look as near as possible to a small perch. He called it, appropriately enough, the Hanningfield lure. So if any perch/fly fishing enthusiasts would like to experiment then I would think it would be a good idea to start with the Hanningfield lure and go on from there. In fact, there is nothing to stop anyone from fishing the Hanningfield lure, or any lure come to that, on a coarse fishing rod and fixed-spool set up, as long as the rules for the water allow it.

When winter arrives perch fishing takes on a completely new aspect. We can forget about shallow lakes and turn to the ones with depths exceeding fifteen feet. Reservoirs are probably the best bet.

Sometimes around the end of October to early November, perch, and some other species, lose interest in feeding. At this time of year the water temperature is falling rapidly and the appetites of fish decrease with it. At a later date, when the temperature has more or less settled to its winter level, the fish become acclimatised and, although not to the same extent as in summer, begin to renew their interest in feeding.

When the frosts have chilled the water to below a temperature of $39.2°$ F. then most fish, including the small ones that perch find so suitably mouth-sized, take to the deep water where the temperature remains constant. All other areas of the lake will continue to drop below $39.2°$ F., so these deep parts, which remain at this temperature, will be the most comfortable. Once the perch have become acclimatised to this, then we can expect to catch them.

Locating fish is without doubt the most important thing we must do before we fish for them. Locating perch in winter is even more essential. When angling for most other species apart from bream we can, at times, afford to err slightly in where we choose to fish, for most other species can be tempted to move a little away from their chosen area by the judicious use of groundbait. Some fish do tend to wander, anyway.

But winter perch have to be pinpointed and to pinpoint them we have to find those deep holes where the temperature remains constant. A boat, of course, would be the best and the quickest way of finding the deep holes, and if you have access to an echo sounder then you can consider it your birthday.

Few of us, however, have access to either, so we must use cruder methods to find the swims. Crude they may be, but what we must bear in mind is that we do not necessarily need to know the actual depth (as long as it is deep enough) but rather to know which areas are deeper than others and, if the contours of the bed are pronounced enough, where the shelves or basins are in these deep areas. A shelf, or a distinct basin in a deep hole, can be considered a hot-spot within a hot-spot, for the big perch still retain their ambushing instinct and can make good use of a shelf or the drop-off into a basin from which to pounce on an unwary victim.

The best of the cruder methods is to use a sliding float, but the disadvantage is the time-consuming altering of the stop-knot on each successive cast. If the reservoir is very large, which they invariably are, then we might find we have to set a full day aside just for the purpose of locating a swim. If the weather conditions are conducive to good fishing, which they are often not in winter, then this time-consuming activity can be annoying, to say the least. We need to take full advantage of good weather for fishing, not sounding.

The method I use, although not as accurate as using a sliding float, is to cast a 1oz bomb and time how long it takes to reach bottom. Alternatively, you can count the number of coils that pull off the spool. Neither way will tell you very accurately how deep the water is, but they will tell you where there is a difference in depth between one cast and another. What you do is position yourself at a specific point and cast directly in front of you, making a mental note of the number of coils that fall off the spool, or the number of seconds it takes before the coils stop falling, and then cast three or four yards to the left and count again. Fan out on each side from that central point on each cast,

145

until you cannot reach the required distance. Then start afresh either further out or closer in. When you have completed the exercise in that spot, move along the bank, to the left say, until your farthest cast to the right will reach to within three or four yards of your farthest cast to the left from your previous central point. Once you find any significant difference in the time it takes for the bomb to drop you can then search the area more thoroughly, now using a sliding float if you like, until you have a reasonably accurate picture of the swim.

Obviously, there is no need to cover the whole lake in this manner, for we can eliminate a great deal of its area simply by studying the lie of the land, and on some first casts from the central point we will find that the swim is too shallow anyway.

Having found a likely swim there are several ways we can go about fishing it. One way is to use a sliding float, but I do not favour this method when fishing in water more than twenty feet deep, which is likely, and especially when I have to cast more than thirty yards, another probability. The stop-knot, whatever kind we use, will restrict casting distance and we would have to use a float with a considerable amount of it showing, particularly in rough water, for us to be able to see it. Again, since we must aim to fish as sensitive as possible a sliding float is not the thing to use in these circumstances.

Legering then, is the answer, either a running paternoster (see Fig. 5) or a link-leger. The rod for this long-range work (which I am assuming it will be, for I have yet to find a good winter perch swim close to the bank) should be about 11ft long with a fairly fast taper for picking up the long line—a line of at least 5lb b.s. because of the heavy weight we will be casting; a fixed-spool reel; a size 6 hook; a swivel, and a bomb of 1oz completes the tackle we need.

Bait can be a small fish, preferably a minnow or gudgeon, or a big lobworm. I usually fish with two rods with a bait fish on one and a lobworm on the other. If I had to fish with one rod and was restricted to one bait, it would be a lobworm every time. Even when fishing two rods, with worm on one and bait fish on the other, I usually find I have a lobworm on both rods after the first two-hour trial period.

The method of fishing a bait fish is very much the same as for

Fig. 5

lobworm fishing, so what I have to say about the one can be applied to the other; except for hooking of course. I always lip-hook a bait fish, for invariably a perch grabs its victim tail first and a small fish like a minnow is easily chomped and the hook is facing the right way to do its job effectively. Some anglers hooking a worm look as though they are practising to be boy scouts. The fancy knots they tie are fantastic; they push the hook through the worm several times until it is buried to the point of being harmless. You should insert the hook about an inch from the head end of the worm, then 'feed' the worm up the hook shank until the point can reappear about half-way down. The worm can then wriggle naturally and look almost the same as it would *without* a hook in it, which is what we should aim for when hooking any bait.

When you cast, always aim to overcast by a few yards; this will allow you to sink the bait on a tight line, which is important. If you fail to overcast and sink the tackle on a tight line the bait will finish up several yards short of the swim; and the deeper the swim, the further away from the swim you will be when the tackle sinks. You could cast directly over the swim and allow the tackle to sink with the bale-arm of the reel open, but this is impractical when you consider that there is invariably a wind on a large, open water, which will cause problems when it grabs hold of a loose line.

When the bomb hits bottom on a tight line, plunge the rod-tip beneath the surface and give a few more turns of the reel to completely and quickly sink the line, to eliminate the effects

147

of wind. This completed, place the rod in two rests with the tip of the rod touching, or slightly under, the surface of the water. Then pull a loop of line from between butt-ring and reel and fold a piece of silver paper over it. Pull the paper to the ground and on the fold place a stone which is just heavy enough to hold it, then open the bale-arm. This will hold the line reasonably tight to the bait and when a fish takes and dislodges the stone the line is free to run for several yards before you strike. You must let it run for several yards, for a perch, however big, usually takes an incredibly long time to completely mouth the bait, lobworm and bait fish alike.

If you have trouble with the perch repeatedly nipping at the worm without taking it properly, grab hold of the line from the butt-ring and snatch it a few times. It can stimulate the perch into grabbing at the worm. If you fail to get any bites at all, reel in a couple of yards every twenty minutes or so until you have covered the whole area. Then re-cast to the far side of the swim and go through the routine again.

Once you hook a perch, take your time with it, not because perch are such ferocious fighters—far from it—but because they cannot adjust their swim bladders to compensate for the change in pressure from the deep water to shallow in the short time it takes to bring them up. I doubt if taking your time bringing a perch up makes a great deal of difference but, coincidence or not, I seem to have many more fish that live to be returned when I bring them in slowly.

The size of the first perch you catch will give you a good idea of the potential of the swim you pulled it from, for perch shoal according to size. If, for instance, you catch a 2-pounder, then it is extremely unlikely you will take one of 3lb plus from the same swim. It would also be very unusual to take a perch of less than 1lb from that swim. If, in these circumstances, you have your sights set on perch of 3lb plus, then it would be a good idea to search for another likely swim and try your luck there.

Whichever swim you fish, unless it is full of small ones of less than 1lb, you cannot expect to take a lot of fish. I cannot explain why, but neither my friends nor I have ever taken more than four or five good perch on a winter's day; not in the depths of winter anyway. In November and early December, yes, when the water was over 40°F., but not in deep swims where the temperature was a constant 39.2°F.

Dick Walker has taken most of his deep water winter perch around mid-day, when the sun was shining brightly and at its zenith, and he reckons it was this light factor, at its strongest water penetration point, that the perch needed to 'turn them on'. Theoretically (and according to Dick's results, which I feel sure influenced his thinking more than theory) it makes sense that perch, who rely greatly on hunting by sight, should feed more when the light penetration is at its greatest.

Unfortunately, I cannot say that my results help to confirm Dick's findings. Although I have had a few around mid-day, most of my deep water winter perch have come in the first and last hour of daylight. This proves nothing, of course, except that perch from one water to another are completely unpredictable. You will just have to see what happens on your own water.

Pike

Pike: a fish that inspires study groups, preservation societies and fanatical followers. A fish that legends are made of; that myths grow from; and the cause of more angler's tales of 'the one that got away' than any other fish.

Wherever you find a water that holds pike you will find an angler who has hooked something that 'felt like a tree'. One who will say, 'I couldn't do anything with it' or, 'It tore off across the lake. I just hung onto the rod until the line ran out'.

You will hear tales of monsters; of leviathans; of ducks and even swans being dragged beneath the surface; of great, vicious heads that poke out of the water to shake the life out of a victim; of swimmer's limbs being mangled; of skin-divers being scared out of their wits. You will hear every monster/maneater kind of tale there is to hear, sometime, somewhere, wherever you find pike.

Even Isaac Walton, writing in *The Compleat Angler*, quoted a certain Gesner as saying that pike are spawned of a weed called pickeral, and implied that he believed Gesner's theory. Walton, however, was a better writer than he was an angler.

In a peculiar way this folk-lore is understandable, for some childhood memories maintain reality into adult life, and the tales we heard and the sights we imagined are not erased easily. The pike, or freshwater shark as it is known, could have been designed in Comic Land to rate alongside 'Tales from the Crypt' and 'The Body Snatchers'. It is a fish that young minds can relate to; can fantasise about; and the tales which have not been heard can be invented and retold so many times that they become reality to the inventor.

150

Let us look at the facts. Pike grow big; the unofficial British record is held by a 42lb 2oz beauty from Norfolk. Pike, like all coarse fish, have teeth; but unlike other coarse fish they have their teeth in their mouths where they can be seen—and felt, if you are careless. They have bifocal vision; eyes that seem to look straight at you; eyes that are set in hard, bony, flat heads. They are mean and vicious in looks, and eat only flesh—mainly of other fish.

They are not our hardest-fighting coarse fish, although they are very good fighters in big, deep, clear waters such as the Scottish and Irish lochs. They are not the hardest fish to catch. Some say they are the easiest and I, for one, would not disagree. They do not scare easily, which is a point in our favour, and they do not demand a great deal of finesse where tackle is concerned. The emphasis on pike tackle is strength; you rarely, if ever, hear of a pike angler having to scale down to get bites, or runs, as they are commonly called in piker's vernacular. It is interesting to note that pike are the only coarse fish for which match anglers do not insist on using light tackle. But I am more inclined to think it is simply a case of the pike being an especially suitable beast to kindle the hunting instinct that lies within us all.

The camouflage colour of pike is perhaps the most effective of all fish. When small and young he spends a great deal of time in marginal rushes and the like, lurking like a motionless tiger in wait for an unsuspecting victim, his green and white stripes blending together in subtle shades that match perfectly the play of light and shade through the rush stems. Later in life the stripes change to a mottled assortment of greens, yellows and whites down his sides, with an almost black back and a white belly. The mottled effect blends perfectly with the trembling light that slants through a rippled surface over deeper water.

The pike is not a hunter but an ambusher, or short-range sniper, hence the excellent camouflage which permits him to lie in wait or stalk his prey without fear of detection. A victim only discovers he is there when a set of sharp teeth clamp across his belly, and then there is little chance of escape. Within the pike's mouth are row after row of needle-sharp teeth that hinge backwards only. Food can slide down towards the throat quite easily, but cannot slide away from it. The larger teeth around the edges of the jaws do the killing; the smaller, hinged teeth, send the food-fish for swallowing after it has been turned lengthways, usually head-first.

Though mainly an ambusher, there are times when the pike has to go in search of food. If he is hungry and he has lain in ambush without a suitable passer-by for any length of time, it is a case of the mountain having to go to Mahomet. Nor does it take him long to find food, for his radar equipment—the lateral line—runs the full length of his body right to the tip of his lower jaw. His sense of smell must be equally acute, for he can home-in on a dead fish with the same swift precision.

The pike is built for short, sharp, sudden bursts of incredible speed. He gets this accelerative power from the anal and dorsal fin which lie far back along the body in close proximity to the tail. One sudden thrust from this rearward propeller and he streaks forward with awesome speed. Rather like a dragster car, he can accelerate tremendously, but cannot maintain the thrust for any considerable distance.

Pike are found in all kinds of waters, from the lowliest farm pond to massive lakes, reservoirs and lochs; from small streams to large rivers. To grow big they need space and, generally speaking, the bigger the water the better the chance of finding big pike. As is the case with all fish, however, there must be an adequate source of food for pike to grow big. The largest water will not produce big pike if there are not sufficient food fish to maintain a progressive growth-rate.

It is the balance of food fish that must be right. There should be sufficient fry to provide young pike with enough food to not only grow, but to grow rapidly. There should be plenty of fish in the 2oz to 4oz class to maintain the pike's growth-rate into maturity, and there should be a good number of fish in the 8oz to 12oz bracket to give mature pike more than enough food to grow big. Finally, there must be sufficient big fish in the 1lb-plus class to ensure that big pike grow even bigger.

Most waters do not have this correct balance of fish, and therefore most waters do not grow big pike. The Cheshire meres, for instance, grow exceptionally big bream and other species, but there are very few fry and fish in the intermediate sizes, and this is why the meres are so poor for big pike. Other waters are over-stocked and swarming with stunted fish of only a few ounces; these also are poor for big pike.

The Norfolk Broads are a first-class example of good pike waters. They have shoals of fry; shoals of fish averaging 4oz, and shoals of larger fish, particularly bream in the 8oz to 2lb class and bigger. They produce plenty of pike of over 20lb every season and not a few 30-pounders.

Then there are other types of waters where the pike grow to truly massive proportions, and in almost every case these waters also contain game fish: trout, sea trout, salmon and, in the case of Loch Lomond, powan. So we can safely say that quality of food is also important.

Pike do eat food other than fish. Worms, frogs, frog spawn, voles, rats, small water fowl and various other creatures have featured at some time or other in a pike's diet. But the use of fish, real or artificial, dead or alive, is the obvious and most productive bait. There are bound to be waters where a bait other than fish, or fish imitation, is more successful, but these waters must be considered for what they are: diversions from the norm; exceptions and not the rule.

There are three basic baits for pike fishing: live fish, dead fish and fish lures which are designed to imitate live fish. Of the three, lure fishing is the least selective for big pike. Only the use of abnormally large lures will ensure that small pike do not make a nuisance of themselves.

Most of the extra-large lures used in pike fishing today were designed and developed in America where lure fishing is far more popular than it is in this country. Whereas our standard equipment consists of long rods, floats and leger weights for bait fishing, the standard equipment of the American is a short rod and a lure, which he uses to catch bass, trout, salmon and pike.

Lures come in many and varied shapes and forms to imitate both real and imaginary fish. There are three basic types: the ones that spin on an axis; the ones that wobble and undulate; and plugs, which either float, sink, dive or rise to the surface according to their design.

Lure fishing is an active occupation in two respects. It involves casting and retrieving continuously as you work the lure through the swim, and it means that you will be moving from one swim to another in search of pike. You could, of course, remain in a likely spot and hope that the vibrations sent out by the lure will be picked up by a pike that passes nearby, and he will come to investigate. But lure fishing, in my view anyway, should be used for stalking fish: you go to the fish, you do not wait for them to come to you.

In a water with plenty of character, such as weedbeds, sunken trees, ledges and deep holes, large boulders, or anything that offers a natural ambushing spot for a pike, it is wise to pass your lure through, or nearby, each of these features in turn until you eventually come back to the first one you tried, and then cover them all again, and so on.

In waters where there is no distinct character you should choose a likely area on the same basis as you would for any fish; a selection based on weather conditions, depth of water, and particularly where you would expect to find a shoal of food fish. Then you should cover the area systematically, based on the well-known clock pattern. You imagine that you are standing in the centre of a clock face and then cast in turn to each figure from 10 o'clock to 2 o'clock. Then you move opposite to either the 10 or the 2 and cast to the same pattern (see Fig. 6). If you have the use of a boat then you can use the same system, only this time you can cover a whole clock-face.

Once you have covered a whole area without a response, change to a different lure for the next covering. Different shapes, actions and colours of lures all have their day. One day you may find that a big, brassy-coloured, violently-spinning lure will be accepted time after time. Other days it will be ignored and a small floating plug, toyed over a weedbed, will be successful.

I do not propose to go into any further detail about lure fishing because, quite frankly, I do not enjoy it, and therefore my attitude towards it prohibits any deep and intimate understanding of its workings. Whenever I use spinning tackle it is usually as a last resort, having failed with all other pike fishing methods. To me, lure fishing, once you have learnt where to cast and how to retrieve at the correct rate, is a mindless exercise in casting that wastes energy that could better

154

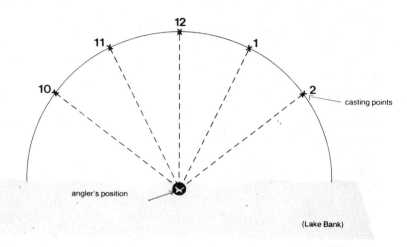

Fig. 6

be spent on thinking. My opinion, however, is biased, and does not reflect in any way on those anglers who do catch big pike on lures. They obviously enjoy lure fishing, and enjoyment is what matters most. But spinning is not for me.

The deadliest methods for catching big pike are with the use of live or dead fish. Which of the two is the more successful depends on the water being fished, for there is no doubt that there are some waters that do not respond to deadbaits, just as there are some that do not respond to live-baits, at least to the same extent as they do to deadbaits. But I must say that I know of far more waters where live-baits are productive than I know of waters where deadbaits have the edge.

Before I discuss bait fishing I think we should first consider the moral aspect of using live fish. I know that, biologically speaking, cold-blooded creatures such as fish cannot feel pain,

155

at least not as we know it. But no matter how convinced we are that sticking a couple of treble hooks into a fish is not painful to them we can never, if we are honest with ourselves, believe that it is not cruel. The definition of cruelty, apart from the infliction of pain, is the intent to produce distress or suffering. That a live fish, tethered like a sacrificial goat in a predator's lair, is distressed and suffering can be taken for granted.

Anti-blood sport supporters are also stepping up their campaign to include angling with fox-hunting, shooting and hare-coursing, all of which involve warm-blooded creatures which feel pain just the same as you and I. Live-baiting therefore only gives them another lever to turn the screw, for we cannot logically argue that live-baiting is not cruel.

At the moment live-baiting is legal and there is nothing to stop anyone from using live fish to catch predators. Nothing, that is, except your own conscience and sense of what is right and what is wrong.

I have stated above that there are some waters which do not respond to deadbaits, but I have experimented on these waters with freshly killed baits fished on live-bait tackle and can truthfully say that my catches have not worsened in any way whatsoever. The baits, however, must be fresh; so fresh you have to take them live to the water just the same as if you were going to fish them live. Just before mounting them on the hooks you tap them on the head.

I have tried, on these live-bait waters, using fish which have been killed the day before and taken them to the water in a polythene bag, but my results do not stand comparison with my results with fish killed on the same day. What I have to say about deadbait fishing therefore includes their use on waters where live-baits are the only consistently productive method, but in these instances the live-bait should be substituted with a freshly killed bait.

What size of bait to use has always been a controversial question, with some experienced pike anglers adamantly saying that a fish of about 8oz to 12oz is big enough for any pike, while other equally experienced pike anglers adamantly state that a really big bait of 2lb or more is more likely to catch a really big pike, and they quote such notable captures as a 40-pounder

A 25lb Loch Lomond pike taken by Graham Marsden on a float-fished
trout deadbait.

from a Midlands reservoir that took a 5lb pike, and the famous
53-pounder from Ireland's Lough Conn that had a 10lb salmon
inside it.

The fact is that the size of bait needed will vary according to
the circumstances. A pike that will readily take a 2lb fish on one
day will, perhaps, only be tempted on a 4oz fish another day. A
lot depends on how hungry he is. I once caught a 17-pounder on
a 2½lb bream on a water where I would not dream of using so
large a bait all the time. Pike of similar size are taken so regularly
from that particular lake on fish of 2oz to 4oz as to make it
worthwhile fishing a small bait on most occasions. The

157

problems involved in getting a really big bait in the right spot and hooking pike on them are not worth the trouble if we can catch them on baits that do not offer these problems. You will find, too, that pike in different waters generally favour a certain size of bait. This size is usually the same as the size of fish which they are used to feeding on and which are most readily captured.

Pike, as far as baits are concerned, are no different to any other fish. Would you think it at all unusual for a roach angler to change to a smaller hook and bait in order to catch fish? Of course not. But it is unusual when pike fishing to try the same thing when bites are not forthcoming. I often think that too much importance is attached to baits. What really matters is the correct presentation of a bait in the right spot. If this is done, then the type and size of bait, to a hungry pike, is largely academic. Note that I said 'a hungry pike', for it is usually only with well-fed pike when the finer points of bait choice become important.

What species of bait to use is another controversial topic. Some anglers swear by freshwater fish, while others say that sea fish are best. Some say it is important to use a bait that is indigenous to the water you are fishing, while others say it is better to use a fish that is different to what the pike are used to seeing. There is no conclusive answer, for each viewpoint is probably correct on the particular water, or waters, referred to.

One of my favourite baits is a dace, and these fish produce pike on the rivers where I catch them and on stillwaters where dace do not live. Grayling, on the same rivers, do not stand comparison with dace. Many times I have hung a grayling under a pike's snout only for it to be ignored. A change to dace has brought an immediate response. But grayling on the same stillwaters where dace are snapped up are also snapped up with equal relish. Perch on some waters are useless, on others they are better than anything else I have tried. This includes waters where perch live, as well as those where they do not. There is no apparent explanation.

Sea fish, particularly sprats, herrings, smelt and mackerel, are usually very good. There are not many waters where these fish are completely worthless. But there are a few waters where runs are very few and far between in comparison with runs you get on freshwater fish. It is also interesting to note that a half-bait can produce twice as many runs as a whole one, which gives rise to the belief that smell is more important, for a half-bait will release more smell from its exposed entrails than a whole, intact bait will. At one time I used to inject my baits with cod-liver oil, but a half-bait has the same effect.

The best bait I have ever used are trout: brown, rainbow or sea, all are equally effective. I have not tried trout on any pike water yet and failed to catch. Of course, I have not always caught at the first attempt, or even the second, but sooner or later a trout has produced a pike. I cannot say the same for any other bait.

Gudgeon, too, are good, and very few waters fail to respond to them. They are, however, open to attack from all sizes of pike, and also from perch, which detracts from their effectiveness when big pike are exclusively sought.

Small baits should not, though, be ignored for sizeable pike. I remember one occasion in particular on a local reservoir, when I and all anglers around me were fishing between us, dace, roach, perch, herrings and mackerel, and not one run had come to any rod all morning. I stuck six minnows on my hooks, one to each point of the two trebles, and landed a 14lb pike within minutes of casting. Then I had a small one of 4lb or so on another six, which was all the minnows I had with me. The moral of that story is, if you have plenty of small baits, then fish a shoal of them.

An excellent bait too, for a big pike, is a small pike. In some waters they really are deadly. On others they seem to be no better than most baits.

There is only one sure way to discover which is the best bait on your water, and that is to experiment when the pike are feeding. Do not, as is so often the case, try a new bait when the usual productive one is catching nothing. The best way is to fish two rods in the same swim, one with a bait which is known to catch pike, and the other with a new bait. If the pike are feeding and either ignoring or paying more attention to a new bait in comparison to their reactions to the known one, then you are able to make a sound judgment. Make sure to experiment with baits fished by the same technique; layed on, suspended etc, or you will not know if it is the bait or the method that is making the difference.

Pike fishing tackle needs to be on the heavy side, not simply because we hope to hook a big fish, but because pike have bony palates, and a deal of punch is needed when striking to plant the hooks. The rod needs to be somewhat stiffer than we would normally use for freshwater fish of similar size. Not only does the rod have to be capable of planting big hooks in bony palates, and strong enough to deal with a heavy fish, but it also has to be able to cast a heavy weight. Even an 8oz bait, which is about average for most pike fishing needs, is too heavy to cast safely and accurately on a 1½lb test-curve rod, which is quite heavy enough to deal with the fish itself.

For most pike fishing situations, when bait fishing at least, those rods of 10ft to 11ft in the stepped-up carp rod classification, are just about right. You need only to go heavier than this when fishing for really big fish in snaggy areas, or when an outsize bait has to be cast some distance.

Reels are a matter of personal preference. Most anglers choose a fixed-spool or a small multiplier. I prefer the multiplier myself, for it is easier to cast a heavy bait on this type of reel, and the free-running spool with the anti-reverse engaged makes run-indication simplicity itself when used in conjunction with a drop-arm indicator, and is especially useful in windy conditions when normal run indicators can be a nuisance. Some anglers favour a centre-pin, which are very good if you are fishing at short range.

Most anglers will use nylon monofil lines of around 10lb to 12lb b.s., which is ample for most pike fishing situations. But you should never hesitate to go heavier when the circumstances demand it. Pike are not tackle-shy, so there is no wisdom or sportsmanship in fishing unnecessarily light. I never go below 8lb b.s., and only use that when fishing waters where the pike are small.

Wire traces are essential, for nylon monofil and any material other than wire is easily severed by a pike's teeth.

When you make your own traces you can mount as many or few trebles on as you wish, or single hooks if you prefer. You can make several with various hook sizes and with both hooks fixed, and with various distances between hooks. Today you can, however, buy some excellent ready-made traces, with both single and treble hooks; barbed and barbless ones. Yet the same manufacturers supply wire, hooks, crimps and swivels to make traces of your own design.

The most popular pike float was the one known as 'The Fishing Gazette Bung'. It was also the worst. It was aquadynamically unsuitable; it is frequently lost because of its poor means of attachment; and the peg was a menace when fishing amongst weeds. It was useless, without modification, for deep water fishing. They are still sold, but only to those who do not know any better.

These days I make my own pike floats from balsa wood. I make them in various sizes in a similar shape to an Arlesey bomb, without swivel of course. A hole is drilled or burned through the centre and a ball-point pen refill tube is glued into it, simply to give the hole a plastic, snag-free lining for ease of line threading. The float is used as a slider with a stop-knot, which enables me to fish any depth of water I need to. You can buy similar ones in both balsa and plastic.

Other items you will need are a large landing net; a gag to hold the pike's jaws open while you remove the hooks—preferably with rubber cushions on the spikes; a pair of long-nosed forceps; and a set of long-handled wire cutters for dealing with deeply-hooked pike. It is better to leave the hooks in after cutting the trace as close as possible to them, rather than trying to force them out.

With most fish you can generalise to an extent as to what is the best time to fish for them. For instance, you can safely say that the dawn period is best for tench on most waters. With pike, however, it is extremely difficult. Of course, there are some waters where you can confidently predict the feeding times, but more often than not pike remain unpredictable. As often as not they will feed at mid-day as they will at dawn or dusk. Just when you seem to have the feeding times on a water 'taped', you find that it has shifted to a different time entirely. Most feeding times last for several weeks, but you can never be certain when it will alter. Not that it matters a great deal if you are in the habit of fishing from dawn till dusk, but it is nice to know all the same. Knowing means you can plan meal times and be extra alert at the right time.

Feeding times, at least in winter, whatever time they occur, are usually brisk and brash. They seldom last for more than two or three hours, and quite often are considerably shorter. But the pike can feed ravenously during this period, and an angler should be prepared to deal with a landed pike in double-quick time and deliver another bait to the water as soon as possible.

When a pike does feed, he usually feeds to his limit—assuming enough food is available—and then fasts for a period that can last for several days. During this period of fast he simply lies practically dormant while he digests the food in his stomach. Very little will tempt him to feed at this time, and you often see a shoal of small fish in his company, each ignoring the other. Even a bait dangled under his snout is usually ignored, and it seems that the only chance you have of tempting him is to aggravate him by jiggling the bait, or by continually drawing a spinner past him. His reaction then comes from anger, not hunger.

Locating pike swims can be, and often is, quite easy, at least on waters which have plenty of character. Pike either hunt or ambush for food, and they make full use of natural cover. Find ledges, weedbeds, depressions in the bottom, sunken trees or branches and, providing these are in a depth of water suitable to the pike in the prevailing weather conditions, here you will find pike.

On featureless waters the task becomes more difficult, as is the case with all coarse fish. Nevertheless, even featureless waters have hot-spots, but the only way of finding them is by fishing trial and error in most areas, until you stumble across one.

These hot-spots on featureless waters are areas where many pike, of all sizes, have packed together, often prior to spawning, but not always. Nobody has yet come up with a feasible explanation for this phenomenon, for there seems to be no logical reason for it: no feature that makes an especially attractive ambushing spot; no shoal of food fish to provide a natural larder; no warmer than usual water to provide comfort. Far more experienced pike anglers than I cannot explain it, so I will make no attempt. Suffice it to say that if you find one of these hot spots, then make the most of it. They don't last for ever.

The best conditions for catching pike are when a westerly or south-westerly wind is chopping the surface, and the open water in this instance is often the best bet. Many pike anglers believe that wind blowing across the open water disturbs the rushes and other unstable cover and forces the pike to move. I am more inclined to believe that the choppy surface breaks up the penetration of light and so provides the camouflage to which the pike's pattern of colours is so suited, urging him to hunt.

Another fact that backs up my thinking is that pike are very often caught well off-bottom when the surface is choppy, for pike could well favour stalking prey at mid-water or shallower when the light is broken up. Their white bellies and mottled sides cannot be easily seen by fish lying deeper beneath them.

A drifting float, carrying a bait about 18 inches to two feet below it, can be cast out and allowed to ride with the waves for a considerable distance. A greased and floating line is essential, or the drag of a sunken line will not allow the tackle to ride along with the waves and will provide too much resistance to a taking fish; it will also greatly impede effective striking.

In the hot-spots I have mentioned, and in specific ambushing areas, such as in the vicinity of a sunken tree, it is usually better to fish with a static bait.

The most common way is to simply 'lay-on' with float tackle, or to leger. But if the bait is still required to fish off-bottom then a paternoster set-up is needed. You have a suitably heavy leger weight at the terminal point and a float at a distance from it slightly more than the depth of water. At whatever depth you want the bait to fish, you tie the trace at this depth below the float, allowing for the length of trace. A three-way swivel is used for the connecting point (see Fig. 7).

You can never be certain at which depth the pike will be feeding from one day to another, so it is wise to vary the depth at frequent intervals, whether fishing a moving or static bait, until you have a run. You may find, on some occasions, that a bait tripping along six inches or a foot off-bottom will be the deadly method above all others. Being prepared to experiment, and not

163

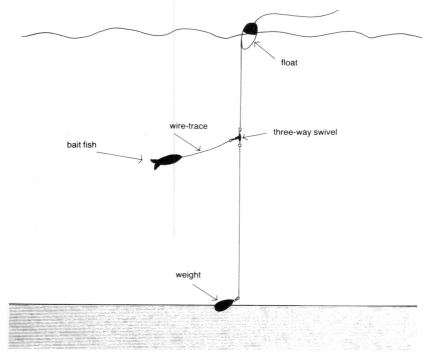

Fig. 7

being set in your ways, is advisable.

Locating pike swims on a river is not a great deal different from stillwater. Finding ambushing spots applies just the same, as does trial and error on featureless rivers. Methods too, are similar, except that trotting the stream can be exploited.

I remember one day's winter pike fishing with Fred Tunnicliffe on the Hampshire Avon at Burgate. I decided to lay-on a patch of gravel behind a dense weedbed. The current was not too powerful, so I used a small float and the weight of a whole herring was sufficient to hold bottom. We had the stretch of river to ourselves, so Fred decided he would trot a herring along the margins all the way down the stretch, walking the bank at the same pace as the bait, from ten yards behind it.

164

Fred Tunnicliffe returns a 21lb pike to the Hampshire Avon. The pike took a trotted herring deadbait.

I had been fishing for some time when I noticed the float bobble slightly; only a minutely different movement than usual, but enough to make me watch it more closely. Every few minutes the float would bobble again, and I was inclined to think it was merely a trick of the current. But no, the float suddenly but slowly swept downstream and I struck into a nice pike of 14lb which, when I landed it, shed the hooks and bait. The herring was not marked in any way and if I had not struck into a fish I would have sworn it had been the current-that was responsible for the tackle shifting.

Only minutes after, Fred shouted for the landing net. He was some hundred yards or so downstream and the bend in his rod suggested he was into a nice pike. He was, and it subsequently turned the scales at 21lb. The remarkable thing was that his float had shot under quite savagely and Fred had struck immediately, but the whole herring was deep in the pike's throat.

So on the same stretch of river, only a hundred yards apart, two pike had taken baits in entirely different ways. One tentatively, and one savagely. No doubt the two different techniques were responsible for the two different takes. The moving bait gave the 21-pounder no time to mess around, while my layed-on bait gave the 14-pounder all the time it needed, and then it only picked the bait up gently.

I sometimes wonder if we are too often responsible for poor pike 'runs', by making it too easy for them when, at times, there is no need for it.

166

Roach

The most sought-after British record coarse fish for some thirty-seven years was the roach.

There are several reasons for this, but perhaps the main reason is the fact that the roach is caught by every angler sometime in the course of his angling life. Familiarity, in this instance, does not breed contempt, but rather an affinity towards the species. If one catches a certain species regularly, the human mind cannot help but speculate about the chances of catching the ultimate specimen, however unrealistic this optimism may be as far as commonsense is concerned.

The record stood since 1938 at 3lb 14oz, a magnificent fish caught by Mr W. Penney. The very weight of the fish, just 2oz short of 4lb, also placed some unusual significance on the capture of a 4-pounder. One often hears and reads those well-worn words concerning the capture of a roach over the 'magic' 2lb mark, or catching one that breaks through a farcical barrier which, in this instance, is again 2lb. So a record that not only doubles a magical figure, but also breaks through three barriers—2lb, 3lb and 4lb—takes on an almost incredible significance. That is, if you believe in magic and invisible barriers.

In 1975, Richard Jones waved his magic wand, broke down all the barriers, and produced a new record roach of 4lb 1oz. The fact that he used a sensible line, a big bait on a big hook, and legered for the fish with some skill in a Nottinghamshire gravel pit, also had something to do with it. Perhaps, now, a record roach will be no more significant than any other record fish. It is sufficient to know that roach of more than 1lb in weight are big fish, and when they exceed 1½lb they can truly be classed as specimens.

Roach are found in all types and sizes of water, from the tiniest farm pond to the mightiest of rivers. Nobody really knows what kind of water grows the biggest roach, for sometimes specimen fish are found in small ponds and sometimes in big reservoirs and rivers. Only a few miles away you can find an apparently identical water where the roach will stop growing at maybe 6oz or 8oz, often even smaller.

Most anglers will never consistently catch big roach, for the simple reason that they cannot resist using tackle that produces lots and lots of small ones. A size 18 hook, sometimes smaller, tied to a 1lb line on which a dust shot is pinched to cock a minute float is thought to be the 'classic' roach set-up. For small roach, it is. Because big roach are hooked on this gear, albeit infrequently, and luck has it the fish is landed, albeit even more infrequently, it is rather difficult to persuade these anglers that such big roach can be caught regularly, by design, with more appropriate, substantial and sensible tackle.

Now and again, you can convince some anglers that they will catch bigger roach more often by changing their approach and using more suitable tackle. But when you mention that they will not get anywhere near as many bites they quickly lose interest. Quality and quantity do not often go together. It is really a question of degree, but generally you must be prepared to sacrifice the one when in pursuit of the other.

I had this lesson brought home to me for the first time some thirty odd years ago when I got quite pally with an old gentleman who used to fish my local canal as regularly as clockwork. He never fished the same swim every week, but I knew that if I walked far enough along the tow-path I would be sure to find him somewhere. He was worth finding too, for I learned a lot from him about fishing, and roach fishing in particular.

In those days the Macclesfield canal, including where it cuts through my old home town of Congleton, was famous for its big roach. Henry was a dab-hand at catching them. If there is any truth in the saying that hungry boxers are the best fighters, then it could be that old Henry was a good angler because he was a hungry fisherman. Part of his catch, whatever the species, always went home for the pot.

I will always remember how I first became friendly with him—if you could call our relationship friendly, for he was a grumpy old so-and-so, outwardly at least. I was fishing 'Bread Length', a very good stretch for big roach if you knew where to find them and how to catch them. I did not, and being only ten years old it was not difficult to find other amusements when the fish were not biting.

I had just thrown a fair-sized cobble at a moorhen, which missed, but splattered into the water with a minor explosion. Up from the rushes popped a cloth-capped head that opened its mouth and shouted, 'What the bloody hell are yer playin' at? Bugger off 'ome if yer can't be quiet!'

'Sorry, Mister,' I said. 'I didn't know you were there.'

There was a stony silence (no pun intended) while Henry probably sulked and no doubt cursed under his breath. I approached him very carefully and quietly, and not a little warily.

'Sorry, Mister,' I repeated. 'Have you caught anything?'

'I aren't likely ter catch owt when you're throwin' bricks in water,' he growled. ''ave 'ad a couple, but don't suppose I'll 'ave any more now.'

'Can I 'ave a look at 'em?' I asked.

He gave me a scathing look and then, surprisingly, pulled his keepnet from the water and showed me two beautiful roach that were well over 1lb each in weight.

'They're nice ones,' I said, unable to hide the awe in my voice. 'What did you get 'em on?'

'Bread. Never fish owt else in th'cut,' he informed me with an air of someone who defies you to argue with him.

'Can I watch you a bit?' I asked.

'No, yer can't. Goin' 'ome now. Time fer pack up.'

The following evening I went looking for him. I took no tackle with me, for I intended just to watch and see if I could learn something. I knew I had the opportunity to discover some of the 'secrets' of catching big fish. That was how I thought about catching big fish then. I had the impression that if anyone consistently caught big fish they had a few secrets up their sleeve that lesser mortals such as I had no access to. It never occurred to me that it was simply the fact that Henry had been fishing a long time; had not been subjected to the brainwashing of the ultra-light-tackle-at-any-cost brigade and had discovered the right approach and technique to catch big roach over the many years he had lived.

I walked along Bread Length again, hoping he would come back to the same swim because of his success there the previous evening. Sure enough, I saw a cloud of blue pipe-smoke billow out of the rushes at the very same spot. I walked along very quietly, not wanting to bring down his wrath again, and crouched silently behind and just to the left of where he sat.

''ad anything?' I whispered.

'Haaaaaawwwwwwkkkkk!' He coughed, almost choking on his pipe. Then he turned to look at me, looked back at his float, and then sent a great brown stream of tobacco juice into the rushes.

'Yer young bugger!' he swore. 'What yer tryin' to do, gimme a stroke? Creepin' about like that!'

'Well you told me to be quiet, didn't you?' I protested.

I remained crouched and just behind him, watching the red tip of the quill float that lay at half cock. I remember being puzzled that it was cast only at the edge of the rushes instead of in the middle where, surely, all big fish are. Everybody knew that big 'uns are always in the middle.

'Why aren't you fishing in th'middle?'

A full minute must have passed and Henry had not answered. Then, just when I was going to repeat my question with youthful persistence, he said, 'Is that where yo' fishes?'

'Well, I try catch big 'uns like you, and big 'uns are always in th'middle aren't they?'

'They're up t'other end o'th'cut when folks like yo' come mitherin' an' makin' a row!' he snarled. I think I was getting on his nerves a bit.

Then his float slid away, and Henry, as though he had all the time in the world, lifted his heavy cane rod with a slightly sharper than usual movement, held the rod still, and simply let the fish plunge under the surface for a few moments. Then he

170

tilted the rod back a little more and the fish, a roach of about 1½lb, slid straight into the landing net which was already submerged at the edge of the rushes. He lifted the net at the moment the fish was securely enmeshed. Then he drew it back until it rested between his hob-nailed boots. The hook was removed and the fish was slid into the keepnet that hung in the water within reach of his left hand.

He pointed to the vee of his rod-rest and said, 'See that? That's what cut looks like on th'bottom, only a bit more rounded. Barges make it like that. Everythin'; all th'muck and mud gets washed up t'th' sides. There's plenty o' snappin' in all that muck and that's what roach feed on.'

'It's not that deep at the side though,' I said, pointing at his float which was set to fish at a depth of at least five feet.

'I know it isn't!' he growled. 'But yer've got 'ave ten inches o' line lyin' on bottom. Yer don't 'ave yer bait danglin' like a bloody yo-yo!'

'Some blokes I know do,' I insisted, 'and they catch a lot of roach.'

'Big 'uns?' he asked, but didn't wait for an answer. He already knew.

I watched him take a pinch of flake from the bread paper at his side, and then squeeze it gently around the shank of the hook, which looked like a long-shanked size 10, leaving it soft and fluffy around the point and barb. I wanted to ask him why he used such a big hook and how he could get bites with such an enormous shot on his line, which was no more than ten inches away from his hook. I wanted to ask him hundreds of things which I could not understand, but I stopped myself, for I could see his neck getting very red, and that told me to keep my mouth shut and ask some more questions another time.

I watched him catch two more big roach (one was not far short of 2lb) in the next hour, and then I went home, looking forward to the next evening when I hoped to find him again and learn a bit more.

It was all very puzzling to me at first. Almost everything he said was contradictory to what I had heard from other anglers. Everyone else I had seen fishing along the canal fished the same as I, with a 1½lb b.s. line, or finer, an 18 hook and a single

171

maggot. Everybody used the tiniest quill float possible, so tiny most carried only a single dust shot. Henry's tackle was crude in comparison.

In the next few weeks I sat with Henry on every chance I got, and I learned that his tackle was not crude at all. Far from it. Certainly not when he explained why he used it, and when the intelligent reasoning and experience that lay behind it became apparent. The puzzles gradually unfolded. It was sometimes difficult to grasp things because of the cantankerous way he explained them, but eventually it did become clear. I began to understand his reasoning when I finally brushed away the uncompromising tactics I had known before. I wondered, too, why it was only Henry, to my knowledge anyway, who had worked it out. Henry's answer to that was, 'Some blokes can't see th'wood fer th'trees.'

Henry was not just the jammy old so-and-so everyone said he was; an old man who was lucky enough to catch big roach in spite of the tackle he used. He was an angler who caught big roach *because* of his tackle, and because he applied what his reasoning and experience told him was right.

He had not fallen into the same trap as I and most others who fished the canal: that to fish light and delicate was always the best way.

Henry taught me that big roach, or indeed, any big fish, are not always 'in the middle'; that big fish are not consistently caught by pure chance, or luck, or whatever one wants to call it. Big fish are caught by knowing their habits and applying your knowledge in the best possible way; not being dictated to by fashion—adamantly using a particular style or set of tackle whatever the situation. He made it clear that substantial, sensible hooks and lines could present a bait to a big fish in a much more natural manner than any gossamer set-up, if that substantial tackle is used in the right way. What was the point, he once asked me, of having a single maggot, or any small bait, on a tiny hook, dangling on a very thin line that was being carried along by the canal's natural movement? It just was not stable enough for big fish. Tackle like that was all right for small fish that fed off-bottom; for fish which are small enough and stupid enough to chase and grab at anything.

A 1lb 9oz roach for Graham Marsden.

Big fish feed on the bottom most of the time he said, so that is where your bait has to be. It has to be held there with a shot that is heavy enough for the strength of undertow and the type of bait. You use a float to suit the shot, and a hook to suit the size of bait, not the other way round.

There was one thing he must have said to me a dozen or more times. Now that I have some experience of my own I know why he repeated it so often.

'Most important thing yer've got to know,' he said, 'is where th'big fish are. Yer can't catch somethin' that isn't there.'

How true that is. Light tackle or heavy tackle, it doesn't matter a damn if you are using it in a barren swim.

So, on that particular canal, the Macclesfield canal, close in to the margins, with your bait lying about two-thirds of the way down the shelf, is the most productive spot for big roach. But this does not mean to say that this is the best place on all canals. The middle, or thereabouts, in the deeper trough eroded by boat traffic, could well be the better spot on some canals. I would imagine that on well populated canals, where pedestrians are frequently making use of the tow-path, the middle section or the far bank will prove to be the best spots.

In other stillwaters, ponds, lakes and reservoirs, roach tend to make use of areas where there is some character. They are a timid fish and grow in sizes that make suitable mouthfuls for pike. Any variation in a water, such as ledges, basins, troughs, weedbeds—particularly bistort and cabbages—and any kind of snag like a sunken branch, offers them some security. These are the places to look for, and the careful use of a plummet on a water you are not familiar with, will help you to locate them.

Roach are a true shoal fish, and like all true shoal fish they usually swim with fish of a similar size. They are not adverse, however, to sharing a swim with another shoal when their paths cross. When this happens the larger roach generally take position on the bottom, with the smaller fish feeding above them. They will, occasionally, share a swim with a shoal of fish of another species, particularly bream, but then you will find that the bream dominate the bottom area with the roach above them.

Big roach do not stay in a swim for any length of time, regardless of the amount of groundbait present in the swim. Thirty minutes is usually the maximum, and then they wander off, only to return perhaps an hour later. This is why there is always a danger of over-feeding roach, for anglers tend to think they have mopped up the groundbait when bites cease after only a short period, and throw more in, in an attempt to persuade them to feed again.

Big roach are wanderers, although their nomadic behaviour is confined to a loose, but nevertheless restricted area which they traverse continuously. Unlike bream, who also follow set routes, but religiously, and only once or twice in a 24-hour period, roach have a much shorter 'beat', but will travel back and forth along this route anything up to twenty times in a 24-hour period. Although groundbait somewhere along the route will interrupt their commuting, it will only do so for short periods; the roach's urge to complete the journey is too strong. As I mentioned, however, it will not be long before they return.

It may be assumed from what I have said that pre-baiting for roach would be of little benefit if it is unlikely we can persuade them to remain in a swim for a decent length of time. But pre-baiting is worthwhile, for two very good reasons. The main one is the same reason we pre-bait for any fish: to teach them to accept our chosen hookbait; to wean them off natural food; to persuade them that our hookbait is tasty, ready and regularly available, and safe.

The second reason why pre-baiting is beneficial to roach fishing is, in fact, to encourage them to spend a longer time than usual in a specific swim. The routes they travel no doubt cover several feeding areas, or hot-spots, and with no interference from anglers the time they spend in each hot-spot will vary very little. But if they continuously find an easily takeable, tasty meal, in one particular spot, then it makes sense to assume that they will spend more time where the pickings are easy than in other swims where they will have to work hard for the same amount of food.

So a single groundbaiting will not encourage them to spend much longer than usual in a swim, but a prolonged pre-baiting campaign can have the desired effect.

The hot-spot along a roach patrol can only be found by trial and error, especially if there is no distinct character on the lake bed to guide you and, unlike bream, roach are not in the habit of rolling to provide us with a clue to the location of their feeding areas. They do show at the surface at times, but I have found that where they show is not necessarily where they feed,

175

although it is a good indication of some point on their beat. It is, however, wise to begin fishing where you have seen them, then to spend some time in swims that branch out from that area, until you find the most productive spot.

My roach fishing is divided about equally between legering and float fishing, although most of my float fishing is trotting on rivers. But I do prefer to float fish on stillwaters where the swims are suitable.

The rod I use with the float is a 13ft carbon match rod, with a slightly more through-action than most match rods. Short rods are not very good for float fishing, especially when using a fixed float in water eight feet deep or more. The extra length is a great advantage when fishing through marginal rushes, for it enables you to reach out and stop the fish from running into the weed along your own bank.

I generally use a fixed-spool reel, but for short-range fishing you can, if you prefer, use a centre-pin in all confidence.

The strength of the line I use depends, as always, on the circumstances, but should be as light as possible. 2lb or 3lb line all the way to the hook is my usual choice, but I do not think twice about using 4lb or even 5lb line if I am fishing near to snags that call for hook-and-heave tactics.

The hook, of course, should match the size of the bait, but I rarely use one bigger than a size 8 for paste, flake and lobworm, and very rarely go below a size 18 for maggots and casters. I prefer a long-shank spade-end hook for bread in all its forms, and short-shank spade-end for most other baits.

Whenever I float fish for roach on stillwater my main concern is for stability, for I believe that big roach are very wary of baits that behave unnaturally, and nothing is more unnatural than a bait that is moving along the bottom, where the water is relatively still, at the same pace as the water movement at the surface. This is exactly what happens when the float is not anchored and is carried along with the surface shift.

On calm days, and especially following a few days of calm conditions, stillwaters really do become almost still. In these conditions you can get away with a very light float which will anchor with no more than a couple of dust shot. But these perfectly calm periods do not happen too often and anyway are not particularly good for feeding fish. Roach, and other fish, prefer some movement in the water, especially when there is a good ripple on the surface. Dissolved oxygen brought about by the movement that begins at the surface is the main reason for their preference, but the camouflaging effect of the ripples breaking up the light also has something to do with it.

My preference, when I have to anchor the bait in an undertow or surfacetow, is for a small antenna float that takes a single AA shot, or, if I need to cast a little further than usual or the water movement is especially severe, for a slightly more buoyant antenna float that will take two AA shot.

Where I place the shot in relation to the hook depends on the bait I am using and the amount, if any, of weed on the bottom, but is usually between six and fifteen inches. I use two shots instead of just one of equivalent weight because two shots will anchor better than one. Both shots are placed together, but I do sometimes pinch another small shot just below the float to sink the antenna lower in the water when I consider this is necessary.

In really rough conditions when I still, for some peculiar reason, want to float fish, I do not hesitate to use a big antenna float that may take two or three swan-shot. Rough conditions, and all other conditions being equal, mean feeding fish, and a heavy but sensitive set-up will not deter roach from biting.

It does not follow that a float of only half the buoyancy, that takes only half the weight of another, is twice as sensitive, for it is not the total weight that fish have to pull, but the amount of buoyancy that is not submerged. The concern in float fishing, as far as weight goes, should not be for what lies under the surface, but for what lies above it. It is what fish have to pull under, or the amount of water displacement, that matters, not what is already under. A big float that is well shotted right down so it needs only one more BB shot to sink it, is more sensitive than a small, poorly shotted float, that needs one AA to sink it.

Of course, we do have to take into account the question of hydrodynamics, in that it takes more force to move a large object through water than it does a similarly shaped smaller one. We would eventually reach a stage where the hydrodynamic force needed to pull a big float and its required shot through water would be greater than the force required to submerge a small tip of float. This is why we should aim to use the smallest float and the least weight possible in the prevailing conditions, but not be fooled however into thinking that the smallest float is always the best.

I use the term 'smallest float' only as a generalisation, for one has to take into account the hydrodynamic shape, buoyancy of materials, finish, etc. In other words, you may have a small float which offers more resistance in water than does a large one with a more suitable design. But if the reader realises what I am driving at by 'smallest float' then this will suffice.

When conditions demand quite heavy float tackle you can take the easy way out and leger. Apart from it being easier there is a lot to be said for legering anyway, where big roach are concerned, for the method presents the bait in a very natural manner while sensitivity is still maintained.

I have a pair of very light, 11ft carbon rods of slightly more than 1lb test curve, which I use for light legering, and they are ideal for roach fishing.

A fixed-spool reel loaded with 2lb line which goes direct to the hook is my usual choice, but I am always prepared to go heavier if I need to fish at long range or in the vicinity of snags.

I favour a light swimfeeder or link-leger for short-range work, usually a link of six to nine inches long, tied to a ¼oz Arlesey bomb at one end and a small swivel at the other. The hook, of course, being a size to suit the bait.

Short-range legering for roach is one of the few occasions when I favour a swing-tip. Not because I am looking for minute twitch bites, for big roach usually bite very boldly, but because I seldom leave the bait lying in one spot for long, and a swing-tip avoids the necessity for continually re-setting the indicator.

It may seem contradictory after what I have said about stability when float fishing, but it is true that if you suddenly snatch the bait along the bottom a few inches it induces the roach to pounce on it. There is, however, a difference between a bait that is slowly being dragged along by a float, and one that moves sharply and unexpectedly every so often. This is the way that most natural live food moves, erratically and a few inches each time, so the snatched bait could be regarded in the same light.

178

I have already mentioned that windy conditions are good for roach fishing, but this is specially so when the wind is blowing from the west or south-west. You should position yourself so that you are fishing into the wind for that is where the roach will be lying.

I remember one winter's day when I was fishing on a local mere. It was bitterly cold and a fringe of ice some six feet wide undulated as the waves from the strong wind lapped into the shore. The wind was in my face and the swim lay about twenty-five yards from the bank. Here it shelved sharply down from four feet to sixteen feet in the space of five yards.

I rigged up a ¾oz fixed paternoster with a size 14 hook and baited with three maggots. I had thrown four balls of maggot-laced groundbait into the swim before I tackled up.

I used a simple dough-bobbin as indicator, and on that day it needed to be a large one, for there was a tremendous pull on the water that steadily made the bobbin rise to the rod. Normally, I would have propped a twig or reed stem on the loop of line that was pulled down between butt-ring and reel, but on this day I could not do so for I had waded out for a few yards and set the rods over nine inches of water. So I had to be satisfied with continually pulling the bobbin back down to an inch or two above the choppy surface.

I fished for over an hour without a bite, or at least without seeing a bite. Then I retrieved one rod and found that the maggots had been sucked. I was at a loss to know what to do. I could not use a lighter indicator, for it was already a constant war between me and the undertow to keep it down. To touch-leger was not the answer, for my fingers were much too cold to feel anything.

What I did do, and I still do not know what my reasoning was behind it (desperation perhaps) was change the size 14 hook for an 8, pinch on a big piece of bread flake, cast in and hold the loop of line down with a piece of dough as big as a pheasant's egg.

No more than two minutes later the dough splattered against the rod and I landed a 1¾lb roach, and six more roach to 1lb 14oz came to my net in the next forty minutes. All to big pieces of flake on a size 8 hook with an indicator weighing six times more than usual that was absolutely smashed against the rod the takes were so savage. After that forty-minute feed I fished on for another five hours but failed to get another bite. My other rod, which was still fishing maggots on a small hook, never had a bite that I saw all day.

On the same water, but this time in summer and fishing from a different bank where the wind was blowing into that day, I took a 30lb bag of roach all between 1lb and 1lb 15oz. I took another 30lb bag the following day, and two days after that I netted 47lb. That period was the only time I have caught roach from that swim, for the wind very rarely blows into that bank. I have tried it many times since, but have never been there when the wind was right. Incidentally, I took six roach of 1lb 15oz in the catches and not one of 2lb or more. Sometimes I wish I was dishonest when I weigh fish. They would have been so much bigger at the 'magic' weight of 2lb!

Roach are very much dictated to by light conditions, and this is very noticeable on rivers when trotting a swim that holds both roach and dace. Roach dislike strong light and do not feed readily when the sun is bright. On the other hand, dace do not mind bright light and you will find that you catch the appropriate fish as the light changes. Roach caught in dace swims are, however, usually a similar size to the dace. Incidentally, the best time to catch roach, on any water, is usually from one hour before darkness, and up to three hours after dark.

Tackle for roach trotting is much the same as the set-up I have described in the dace chapter for dace trotting (page 120). It is advisable, though, to increase the breaking strain of the line by about 1lb and to shot a little heavier nearer to the hook, so that the bait follows the bottom more determinedly.

Big roach tend to hug the sides in a river, and where you find overhanging vegetation, specially hawthorn and elderberry bushes, over a very slow glide, or even a virtual slack, you will usually find big roach.

When you have to cast the bait so close to the far bank you should try to choose a swim where there is an opening between the bushes, otherwise you will snag more often than not. If you find a gap just above the swim you can cast without fear of snagging and trot the tackle into and through the hot-spot.

A 7¼lb roach x bream hybrid Graham Marsden caught on a Cheshire mere. Possibly the biggest roach x bream hybrid taken in Britain.

I much prefer, however, in this instance, to fish from the same bank the swim lies. It is a simple matter then of dropping the tackle under your feet and much easier to keep it tucked right into the bank. If the vegetation will allow, you should use a long rod so that when a fish is hooked you can pull him away from the bank and let the playing take place towards the middle of the river. It is easier, too, to feed the swim with accuracy and without waste, unlike feeding a far bank swim which inevitably means the feed will not be so concentrated, with some of the 'spread' escaping the swim.

I know quite a few roach swims such as the ones I have described, where there is not a big enough gap through which to cast float tackle and where I am not allowed to fish the far bank. In this instance the only answer is to leger. Even so, casting through these narrow gaps takes some doing, and I resign myself to the fact that I am going to lose some tackle. It does not deter me though, for this kind of fishing has a fascination all its own and the reward of a big roach or two make it worthwhile.

181

When the gap you have to cast through is no more than a few inches you have to assemble the tackle so that free-swinging line is kept to a minimum. By free-swinging line I mean the line from stop-shot to hook. The shorter this line, the less likely it is to snag on the branches as the leger weight passes through the gap.

I generally tackle up with a running bullet which I have fitted with a swivel. This is stopped about four inches from the hook when worm, maggot, or caster fishing, or one inch if I use crust. Avoid using a swing- or quiver-tip, for these contraptions only interfere with smooth and accurate casting. Touch-legering in this instance is much better.

If the river is narrow enough, the best technique is what I call the pendulum cast. It simply means you swing the end-tackle like a pendulum back and forth towards the gap, slowly gaining momentum, and release the line at exactly the right moment on the forward swing, and then brake the tackle by dropping your finger onto the lip of the spool as the tackle reaches the swim. Once you make a really good cast that lands exactly where you want it, then leave it there for even longer than you would in an unrestricted swim. The more often you cast, the greater your chances of snagging, and snagged tackle can mean disturbing the swim when you free it, which in turn can lead to an even longer wait for a bite than if you had left it there in the first place.

The branches that surround the gap you are casting through will more than likely trail right into the water. After the tackle has hit the swim you should then sink the rod-tip well down so that the line sinks quickly and is not carried into the snags. This is another reason why swing- and quiver-tips are, in this case, useless, for you can leave the rod-tip under water when touch-legering.

It is not often you will catch a good net of big roach from these swims, specially on small, narrow rivers. But the sheer pleasure of extracting only one from this, or any other skill-demanding situation, is ample reward.

Rudd

If you like beauty and colour in a fish then you will like rudd. There are several variations in colour of these fish, but the most common is the brilliant red-finned one. These have greenish-blue backs, silver flanks in the smaller sizes which changes to a handsome bronze when they get bigger, and those startling red ventral, anal and tail fins. Just to add a final dash of colour, the iris of the eye is yellow. The next most common rudd has yellow underfins, and you can find this variety in the same water as the red-fins. You are unlikely to find the other two varieties, the red and golden rudd, in natural waters.

The rudd can, to the inexperienced eye, easily be confused with roach. But once you can distinguish between the two, recognition is simple, for the rudd is deep-bodied with the dorsal fin set behind the pelvics. The bottom lip of a rudd protrudes, unlike the level lips of a roach. Finally, there are the brilliant red underfins and the yellow eye.

It is a small species, growing not much bigger than roach. The record stands at 4lb 8oz, but any rudd over 2lb can be classed as a good specimen, and 3-pounders are a rare prize. They are found in all manner of stillwater, from tiny farm ponds to large reservoirs, and in some slow-moving rivers.

Although I have caught plenty of big rudd from small ponds of no more than half an acre in area, I would never risk stocking rudd into a small water. Like Crucian carp they are very prone to over-breeding, and in an incredibly short time they can reduce a good mixed fishery to one that contains little else but stunted rudd. Unlike Crucians, however, which seldom, if ever, reach specimen size in small waters, rudd often do. But it is as well to let nature decide which small waters are suitable for big rudd; man too often makes the wrong decision.

Rudd are surface feeders, which is why they have been given a protruding lower lip to facilitate sucking insects and other food through the surface, but not exclusively so, for at times they feed right on the bottom and frequently at all levels from the bottom to the top. Although they can, and do, take food right off the bottom, I am sure they prefer to get below a bait, which means they are assuming their most comfortable feeding position. I have lost count of the number of times I have caught rudd while fishing for other species on the bottom, but most of the bites came within seconds of casting, which indicates that the rudd were taking 'on the drop'. I dare gamble that most rudd supposedly taken hard on the bottom have grabbed the bait before it has even settled. Simply because one fails to get any indication does not mean that the rudd has not taken.

Even when legering this could be the case, for most leger set-ups have a hook-length, or tail, of at least twelve inches, which continues to fall slowly, especially with a bread bait, after the leger has hit bottom. I have had the line snatched from my finger while setting an indicator more often by rudd than any other fish.

Rudd are shoal fish, and quite often you will see a large area of a lake being disturbed by a shoal of priming rudd. You will see this disturbed area moving slowly with the drift of the surface as the rudd follow *en masse*, the insects being carried along with the drift.

They are summer species and thrive quite happily in water temperatures so high that most other species are lying immobile in shaded area. But after late September they lose interest in food, and even in the deep water of a lake where the temperature is a constant 39.2°F., they are rarely caught.

Rudd love shallow water too, which is understandable considering that most of the creatures they feed on breed in shallow water. Even six inches of water is not too little at times, but it would be too difficult to catch more than one fish from such a depth after the inevitable disturbance. Depths of two to four feet are ideal for rudd, and ideal for us to catch them from.

Graham returns a 2lb 9oz rudd.

Those rush- and reed-fringed lakes and meres are usually excellent big rudd waters. Quite often they are inaccessible from the banks, but the use of a boat means we can enjoy some marvellous sport, for we can cast towards the fringes rather than through them, following the rudd around when they are keeping pace with surface drift.

A 12ft or 13ft match rod is the ideal weapon, coupled with a fixed-spool reel loaded with at least 2½lb line. You need a fairly substantial line to bully the rudd away from the rushes and get them into the landing net as quickly as possible. There is no point in letting the fish have its own way, for if it is allowed to plough around the swim it will scare the whole shoal away.

Hooks should be fine-wire spade-ends, a size 12 or 14 for a

185

bunch of maggots or casters, and a 10 or 8 for flake and crust. Worms are a useful bait too, but I have never known rudd to refuse maggots, casters or bread, so it is your choice, rather than the rudd's.

My choice of float is a simple piece of peacock quill. I cut off a piece bigger than I need, bunch (right under the float) as much shot as is required to cast where I want, drop the lot over the side of the boat, and then cut the float down with a sharp knife a bit at a time, until I have as much float sticking out of the water as I can see easily.

The two ways of attaching the float both have advantages and disadvantages. If you attach it bottom rubber only—'peg-leg', as this style is known—it means you will have few tangles when casting but the float can more easily snag in the rushes, for we must cast as close to the rushes as we can, even in the gaps between them. The other way is to attach the float top and bottom with rubbers that extend slightly over the tips of the quill (see Fig. 8). This way it will not easily snag in the rushes, but will tangle pretty often when casting, the trailing hook catching on the line above the float.

The double-rubber method would be the best if the bulk of the shot is not bunched right under the float. But we want to make the float lead the way when we cast, so that it will enter the rushes and the bait will sink slowly behind it. I think, however, the double-rubber method just has the edge over the peg-leg method.

I have found that a bait fished from six to eighteen inches from the float is sufficient. Any deeper and the bait will be sinking too far away from the productive area: too far behind the float, that is.

If you are fishing with bread then a very light mix of cloud groundbait is ideal. You must throw or catapult it in, in small balls only, say no bigger than a golf ball, for the rudd will be at or near the surface and big lumps of groundbait are more likely to frighten them off than to attract them.

Most often I do not use groundbait for this type of rudd fishing. I prefer to catapult pinches of hookbait, either squeezed flake or damp crust, into the swim at frequent intervals. The only time I use groundbait is when there is a very big shoal and

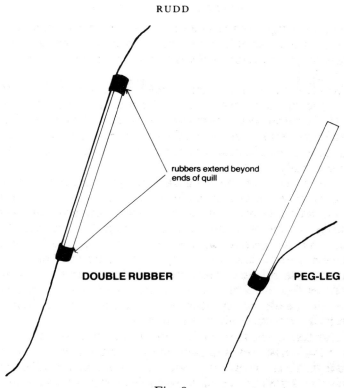

rubbers extend beyond
ends of quill

DOUBLE RUBBER   **PEG-LEG**

Fig. 8

pinches of flake would not be enough to keep them interested, at least not without spending half your time feeding the swim and so losing half of your fishing time.

When using flake or crust as bait you do need a small shot to pull the bait under the surface, but this should be only just heavy enough to do the job, for a slow-sinking bait that the rudd can seize while it is still sinking is an essential element of the method. In any case, a heavy shot may counter the weight of the bunch of shot under the float which we need to ensure the float leads when cast.

Maggots and casters are the best baits of all for this style of fishing. Not for the reason that rudd are more partial to these baits than any other, but because we do not need any shot whatsoever down the line. A bunch of maggots or casters will sink under their own weight, and you can easily feed as few or as many as you wish into the swim without disturbing the fish.

Fly fishing for rudd can be deadly too, and there are not many patterns of dry fly they will not take. Alternatively you can fish with a bright lure on a part-sunken leader. Lures imitating perch fry are especially good. If your tackle does not run to a fly fishing outfit you can just as easily use fly fishing lures on a spinning outfit, and some small, brass-coloured spinners are worth a try too.

Many times you will be faced with a situation where it is impracticable or at least difficult to float fish for rudd. There may be no boat in the water and the fish too far out to reach them with float tackle. You may want to fish for them in darkness, and again the fish are too far out for you to be able to see a betalite tip or a float with a torch beam on it. Whatever the reason, you will encounter situations where legering is the only sensible way of fishing. Indeed, very often I choose to leger even when float fishing is possible, for you can do some things with a leger set-up which you cannot do at all, or at least as well, with float tackle. One of these is fishing with a bait that rises from the bottom.

I remember one rudd-fishing session in particular where legering for them paid off very handsomely. It was on a beautiful Cheshire mere not far from where I live. About fifteen acres in area and very shallow, it holds a good head of tench and not a few rudd that grow to over 3lb.

I would love to spend more time on the water myself and make a special, prolonged effort, to get to grips with one or two of those huge fish. The difficulty, at least from my point of view, is that the mere is only available for fishing by booking well in advance; throughout the summer months anyway. The reason for this is that the pool is a bird sanctuary and only open to fishing along one short stretch of bank. Only a handful of anglers are allowed to fish at any one time, and the majority of anglers who fish the mere, despite its enormous potential for big rudd, go all out for tench. Who can blame them? The tench are easy to catch and there are plenty of them to about 4lb. No special preparations or tackle are needed to catch these tench, and this counts for a lot on a pool which you can fish only occasionally.

I have enjoyed many an evening on the pool myself, usually catching up to a dozen tench in two or three hours. Great fun, but when I have managed to drag my eyes away from the bubbles that surrounded my float and seen the dimples and swirls further out on the mere, where rudd were sucking insects off the top, I have vowed to ignore the tench sometime and make a special effort for those big redfins.

I made my plans to fish there and I had already discarded the idea of float fishing, for although the odd rudd is taken from this particular mere whilst float fishing, they are just that: odd fish that rarely approach the size of some of the rudd that can be seen priming much further out than a long float cast. If an all-out attack on the rudd was intended it would have to be by a method that would avoid tench and encourage rudd.

Some form of legering had to be the answer. Several legering techniques occurred to me, all having one thing in common: they would allow the bait to be fished at any level, including the surface, providing, in most cases, a buoyant or semi-buoyant bait was used. The ideal bait is crust, or balanced crust, which is simply crust with just enough paste around the shank of the hook to let the combination sink slowly.

The ideal bait was a balanced crust on a free-line rig, but a bait of this nature that would be heavy enough to cast the distance necessary, without the aid of a weight, would have been much too big for even the biggest rudd. Big rudd can, and do, take very large baits that are meant for carp, by whittling the bait down to a manageable size, but I wanted to catch them with a bait off-bottom, not with a bait that lies still on the bottom giving them all the time in the world to carve it up.

Fishing a crust with the aid of a weighted bubble float would have been of little use. For one thing, the water fowl on the pool would not allow a crust to stay at the surface long enough for a rudd to find it. Again, I wanted to start just before dusk and fish an hour or so into darkness, and there is little hope of seeing a float in that kind of non-light. I would have to use a bite indicator at the rod end so I saw no point in encumbering my end tackle with unnecessary flotilla.

It was obvious that I would have to use something that would allow a crust to rise off the bottom, rather than sink from the top. The easiest and simplest way, normally, is to use an ordinary running leger and allow the crust to pull line through the swivel until it reaches the required level. Normal circumstances were not the order of the day though, for this mere, most seasons, is plagued with filamentous algae, and this was one of its worst years. A terrific explosion of the stuff had occurred.

This weed, a real angler's curse, looks just like green cotton-wool. It breaks off the bottom, most of it rising to the surface, and the rest 'hovers' at all levels beneath the surface. Wind and rain are the only elements that help. Wind drives the surface weed towards one bank, leaving clear patches to fish through, and rain, heavy rain that is, breaks it up and also creates clear patches.

The great volume of algae that floats on the surface like an aquatic carpet is not the only problem. Simply because a particular surface area is clear, allowing tackle to enter the water unhindered, does not mean the problems are over. Far from it, for the millions of tiny particles that hang suspended at all levels beneath the surface are just as great a headache.

The particles virtually rule out using any kind of running tackle. They cling to the line and swivel, and once the line begins to run through the swivel an enormous build-up occurs. More and more algae accumulates in the eye of the swivel as line is drawn through until, after only a few inches of line have passed, the whole lot seizes up solid. It does not need much imagination to see what effect this can have on a taking fish. So that ruled out the use of any form of running leger.

The only answer was a fixed paternoster. This entails having a leger at the terminal end of the main line and a hook-length short enough so as not to hang below the leger, tied back up the main line. This set-up would allow me to cast the necessary distance; it would have nothing running that could clog and terminate the run, and would allow me to fish at all levels from bottom to surface.

Once I had decided what to use I became rather excited at the prospect of fishing the mere for those big rudd. On the way to the water that evening the only thing I had any qualms about was the difficulty of finding a clear and vacant area, for the weather had remained dry and calm and there was little prospect of the algae being less of a problem than of late. In fact, as far as the algae was concerned, the conditions had worsened, with heatwaves robbing the air of freshness and feeding the weed with life-giving sun-rays. I feared the worst.

I thought my fears were proven right when I first arrived, for the car-park was almost empty and the usual swims were covered with a green carpet that looked like a well-kept bowling green. Miserably, I walked the bank to its limit and there, right at the end, was a wide clear area that reached almost to the opposite bank. There was enough space for two anglers.

Then I noticed why no-one else was fishing there: over-hanging branches made it impossible to cast from the margins. Wading out to beyond the overhanging branches was the only way to make an unrestricted cast, and this meant you were only a few yards away from where you would normally float-fish for tench. Since it was my intention to fish for rudd at a range of forty yards the wading would have no effect on my fishing. Thankfully, I sat down to think before I began to fish.

Groundbait was essential, both to attract the rudd to the area and also to encourage them to stop and feed for a while. Groundbaiting in the ordinary way, with compact balls of crushed bread that would break up on the bottom, was no problem. The question was how to bait the swim at all levels from the bottom upwards. One way would have been to catapult out a few crusts that would float on top, and a few pieces of pinched flake that would sink slowly.

But that would have been a successful way only on a water that did not have the wild fowl population of this mere. The splash of groundbait balls breaking through the surface is the signal for all sorts of feathered pests to knock hell out of each other as they battle for the prime pieces that remain at the surface long enough for them to get at it. One peculiarity about the mere's bird life is that they very rarely dive for groundbait once it has reached the bottom. It may be because of the thick algae, or it could be due to them having been hooked so often when stealing anglers' baits off the bottom.

Whatever the reason, they rarely hang about for long once they have cleared up the floating tit-bits—especially when a ¾oz Arlesey bomb explodes only inches away from their grabbing beaks.

The answer to groundbaiting lay in the same direction as the answer to fishing a buoyant bait: to come off bottom. It was a simple matter of poking dry crusts into the stiff balls of groundbait and then, as they began to break up on the bottom, the crusts would slowly float to the surface. The time between the groundbait hitting the surface and the balls dissolving would be time enough for the birds to have a quick snack and clear off before the crusts came floating up within reach of greedy beaks.

This I did, and it worked like a charm. Within ten minutes of the groundbait going in crusts started popping to the surface, sometimes one, sometimes more, continually appeared as the groundbait dissolved. The beauty of it was that the swim, from the bottom upwards, was being fed little and often.

I set the hook-length on the main line some three feet back from the bomb; the hook-length itself being six inches long. The swim was three feet deep, so this meant I could fish a buoyant crust six inches from the bottom, through all levels up to the surface, simply by tightening the line to hold the crust down or releasing line to allow it to rise to any desired level (see Fig. 9).

The hook was a size 6; big enough to hold a crust of suitable size and buoyancy, yet not too big for rudd in the 2lb plus class. Line was 4lb b.s., and the bomb ¾oz.

I cast, and sat back in readiness for the first signs of action, and it was not long before I saw the tell-tale dimples and the occasional swirl at the surface that was unmistakably rudd. They were at the edge of the vast blanket of algae some fifteen yards to the left of the swim. Then the dimples and swirls gradually approached the baited area and the swirls became more dramatic as crusts were tweaked at and sucked into hungry mouths. These were the crusts that had slowly drifted towards the algae, but soon several fish were evident over the swim itself.

I took the dough-bobbin off the line and let the line run through the rings until all the slack was taken up. Now the crust

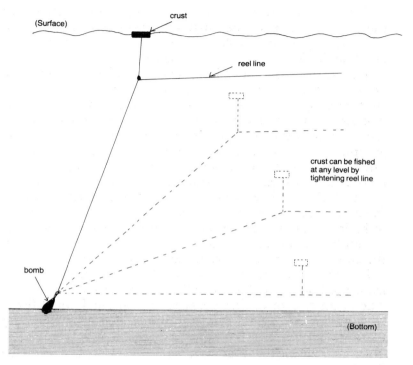

Fig. 9

was at the surface. I pulled another twelve inches of line from the reel and pinched on another, much smaller bobbin. Or, I should say, tried to pinch on a smaller bobbin, for the line was snatched from my fingers with a viciousness typical of big rudd. I hooked the fish, or it hooked itself (not that it mattered), and landed a nice rudd of 1½lb.

I took two more rudd from the surface before everything went quiet. So I pulled the crust down to six inches off-bottom and held it there with a heavy bobbin. Nothing happened. Next, I let the crust rise another six inches and held it there. Still nothing. I released another six inches and again the line was snatched from my fingers. A rudd of 2lb 2oz joined its mate in the keepnet. During the next forty-five minutes I took seven more rudd just by letting the crust rise slowly from the bottom and waiting for line to be whipped from a finger-tip.

It may sound silly, but every time that line was suddenly snatched away, I had a minor heart attack. Although I was expecting it, it still came as something of a shock (anglers who regularly spin for pike will know exactly what I mean). Probably not with half the shock, however, that the eleven rudd experienced when they found themselves hooked. The first fish of 1½lb was the smallest, six were over 2lb, and the best was 2lb 9oz.

I have used the method just described many times since, even when there has been no weed to hamper anything, and taken plenty of good rudd. When there are crusts rising continually from groundbait on the bottom it is only natural that a rising hookbait offers the best chance of catching fish.

Tench

We anglers tend to slot fish into two brackets, summer species and winter species. This does not mean that summer fish cannot be caught in winter, or vice-versa, but that we generally set out to catch a species at the time of year it is most likely to be taken.

If we needed a perfect example of a 'summer fish' we need look no further than the tench, for he is a voracious feeder in the opening two or three weeks of the season and gradually sinks into oblivion as each passing month brings a drop in water temperature. Of course, there are instances when he is caught in winter, but these are so rare they are not at all typical of the species.

There are two months, one of each season, which mark the traditional beginning of a period when a species is fished for. One is October, when anglers begin to pike fish in earnest. There is no logical reason why October should mark the start of the piking season, except for ancient bye-laws and out-dated thinking, but 16th June, which traditionally is the start to the tenching season, makes good sense, for there are more tench caught in June and early July than any other months. Not, as might be supposed, because there are more anglers fishing for them at that time, for any experienced tench fisher will tell you that they are a lot easier to catch in June and early July. They are usually bigger, too, full of spawn and swollen, as was the current record of 12½lb.

There are several reasons why tench are so much easier to catch in the early season. Perhaps the main reason is because they have had so long to forget about the dangers of anglers' hooks and baits, for whereas most fish only have three months close season, a tench feeds very rarely, if ever, from October onwards, and this means he has not sampled an angler's bait for seven or eight months. The other reasons are higher water temperatures and the forming of huge schools which feed ravenously in preparation for spawning, which usually takes place at the end of June or the beginning of July, even later when the water temperature is not quite right by that time.

One often hears of tench being described as shoal fish, but I do not believe that they are in the truest sense of the word. To me, a shoal fish is a species which always spends its life in the company of fish of its own kind, be there a dozen big ones or hundreds of small ones. Shoal fish move and feed as a unit, like a regiment of soldiers that act with a single mind, automatically and without question.

I rather think tench live in what I can best desecribe as families, usually three to five females and one male. I know one often sees twenty or thirty tench together, sometimes more, and one often has a large number of tench feeding in a swim, but I believe this is mere coincidence, when separate families happen to come together because they all happen to be going that way at that time, or, as in the case of a baited swim, all have met there for the same reason—to feed. Once the business at hand is finished, or the coincidence passed, the families go their own way, which is why you more often see small groups of tench than you do shoals.

Quite regularly, when fishing for tench, you will notice that you catch fish spasmodically. You can catch several fish one after the other, then nothing for a period, then several more one after the other, and so on. I believe this is a case of a family of tench moving into the swim, being caught, then followed by a succession of other families moving in. When we have a large number in the swim at the same time it is probably because we began fishing after all the families had gathered, or they had gathered before they got to the baited pitch and then moved in all at once. At the appropriate time the tench could have shoaled anyway, in readiness for spawning, and you happen to be fishing in the designated area.

I have spent hours watching tench, mainly in these small groups, and have been amazed at some of the tricks they get up to. They remind you of small children, for they chase each other as in a game of 'touch and run'; do acrobatics; perform rituals reminiscent of the foreplay of animals before mating, and all manner of things that seem to have no reasonable motive apart from play. Tench have runs through weed, small tunnels that remind one of rabbit burrows, and they spend hours passing through these burrows, sometimes chasing each other quite viciously. I often wonder if this is one tench defending his territory against another, which is quite feasible when you remember that most, if not all animals, are territorially minded.

Tench are bottom feeders and this is where we mainly fish for them. But in lakes which hold surface-feeding fish like rudd and carp they are not adverse to copying. One lake I fish now and again holds a tremendous head of carp, mostly small ones where a 50lb plus net of fish is the rule rather than the exception. Any method will catch the carp but I get more fun out of them when I employ floaters. So do many other anglers, which is why there are always a lot of floaters around on the surface. Here, as many tench can be caught at the surface as is possible off the bottom. This is just another illustration that tench and other fish can be educated both to the advantage and disadvantage of anglers. The anti-pre-baiters should bear it in mind.

Tench, like bream and other basically bottom feeding fish, are covered in a layer of mucous. This slime is a protection against the bacteria and parasites which live in the bottom mud and would be only too willing to use tench as hosts if they got the chance. As evidence that tench are more adaptable to bottom feeding there is the fact that the mucous of tench is much tougher and adheres to them far more readily than to other fish. Although they look and feel much slimier than other species, they are in fact far cleaner to handle for the simple reason that the slime does not come off onto your hands in quite the same way.

The colouring of tench, apart from uncommon deviations from the norm, ranges from a light green to bottle green, and from a light bronze to almost black. The lighter-coloured fish are usually found in lakes which have very clear water and perhaps a sand or gravel bottom; the darker ones are usually found in black mud-bottomed lakes or a lake where they

197

habitually live in deep water. It is all a question of camouflage and their colouring is adapted to suit their usual background. Move a tench from one type of environment to another and it will not be long before its colour changes to suit.

As far as the power league goes then tench belong in division one, somewhere near the top. Their bodies are almost cylindrical, torpedo-shaped, small-headed, red-eyed and extremely solid and muscular. Their fins are big paddles which give them tremendous power, and the wrist of the tail is very thick, the tail itself like a big spatula giving them a burst of speed that is difficult to reconcile with the docile expression on their faces.

The male of the species is a smaller fish than the general run of tench in a fishery and he can be recognised by the massive pectoral and ventral fins that look much too big for his body. These extra-large fins give him a tremendous burst of speed and power that belies his size and it can be disappointing to discover that a tench you were convinced was exceptionally big is, in fact, a modest-sized male. Tench are the only coarse species where the male and female are easily distinguished by the layman.

Tench are widespread from the south to the north of England and can be found in reservoirs, lakes, meres, small ponds and even tiny farm ponds. They are very tenacious and can survive for long periods out of water, and when a natural hazard such as pollution and deoxygenation of a fishery occurs they are usually the last species to die. They are affectionately known as the 'doctor' fish, supposedly possessing magical medical powers. Feeble this may be, but it is certainly true that they know how to look after themselves.

I am not a great advocate of laying down temperature feeding ranges for fish, for so much depends on conditions preceding the time when they come on or go off feed. We can only generalise and a range from 60–70°F. is the usual bracket into which tench are slotted. It is well worth remembering though, that tench are more likely to feed at a rise to 58°F. following an unusual cold spell, than they are at a drop to 60°F. following a warm spell. If you use a thermometer you can keep track of these rises and falls in temperature and use the knowledge to your advantage.

198

Subtle rises and falls in temperature have a much greater effect on tench, as far as feeding goes, than any particular figure on the temperature scale. A rise or fall, depending on the preceding conditions, can switch them on or off. If I had to choose a specific temperature at which tench are at their best in feeding terms I would go for 68°F. We will not be far out if we judge that tench are likely to feed if the temperature is moving towards that figure—rising or falling—and unlikely to feed if it is moving away from it—rising or falling. A steady temperature can also be taken as a good sign, but so much depends on other factors we can only generalise and choose which rule of thumb we apply to the effects of temperature.

One of those other factors that have a great bearing on whether or not tench will feed is light. They usually dislike strong light and the light that most penetrates water is the one that comes from directly overhead: a mid-day sun. Late evening, through the night, and early morning before the sun rises more than 10° are the times of least light and when tench are most likely to feed. Conversely, tench in many gravel pits feed when the light is at its brightest.

By far the best period of all is early morning. There are usually more tench caught at this time than the whole of the night and late evening put together. But why should this be so? If it is true that tench dislike strong light then the opposite end of the scale is surely almost total darkness, which is through the night. We have to ask ourselves then, what does the early morning offer that the late evening and night does not?

The main, and only really significant difference, is that there has been a drop in temperature and a reduction in the amount of dissolved oxygen in the water, for plants give off carbon dioxide in darkness and this has reached its peak by the time dawn breaks. Tench, although they can tolerate less oxygen than other fish, do not necessarily get 'turned on' by the lack of it. But tench undoubtedly love weedy water, and a great deal of weed could inject a surplus of dissolved oxygen into a water during the day, which is reduced to a comfortable amount by early morning when the plants have finished breathing through the night. Combine this with a drop in water temperature, which could be a good thing in June or July when there is every chance the afternoon temperature reaches more than 68°F., and with a lack of strong light you have ideal conditions for tench to feed.

As the day wears on and the sun reaches higher in the sky the tench's appetite decreases at the same pace, until, usually around 9.30 a.m. in June or July, they cease feeding altogether or move off to deeper water where the light cannot penetrate to the same extent. On cloudy, dull days, it is not unusual for tench to feed throughout most of the day, although the periods between each feeding spell, or group of fish moving into the swim, will grow further apart as the day grows older.

It is quite easy to select a good tench swim once we know what to look for. We know they have a profound liking for weed (I include all types of aquatic vegetation in this loose term) and that most tench waters have the bulk of this weed around the margins. Tench also send up bubbles when they are feeding on the bottom, even in hard-bottomed lakes and pits which have a thin layer of silt over the gravel, clay or sand.

These bubbles are extremely minute, no bigger than the head of a pin. Once you know what they look like they cannot be mistaken for gaseous eruptions from the bottom, or the bubbling of other species. When there is a lot of tench in the swim the surface can be a mass of these tiny bubbles and when there are only a few tench present you will see patches of them here and there as each tench delves into the bottom.

Lilies are not a particularly beneficial plant to a fishery, giving little in the way of oxygen and little else in the way of food, but tench are very attracted to them, mainly, I think, because of the sense of security and shade the floating leaves, or pads, offer. If we choose a swim in the vicinity of lilies, or even in the midst of those sparsely scattered ones, particularly if we have spent some time merely watching for bubbling tench and seen their distinctive bubbles in the area, we will not go far wrong.

Pre-baiting for tench is very beneficial and, where the bottom is of the right type, raking is also a deadly way of attracting tench to an area and inducing them to feed. Raking means just what it says, to rake and disturb the bottom, causing clouds of mud releasing the tiny creatures that tench normally root for in the mud. What you are doing is giving them a meal on a plate

Graham Marsden and Eric Barnes with tench over 5lb.

instead of them having to seek food for themselves. A combination of the two, raking and baiting, is especially effective, and I have found the best way is to groundbait first and rake afterwards. This method mixes the groundbait and hookbait samples with the mud and looks much more natural when everything has settled again. It also forces the tench to work harder for the feed instead of merely picking it off the top. Having to work harder means they will have to spend more time in the swim, which in turn means more time for us to catch them.

It is risky, however, to rake a lake bottom when you are not sure of the composition of the bottom. In an area where there are a lot of trees which have shed their leaves in the water for many years the bottom, if disturbed, stinks absolutely foul and will only result in driving the tench away rather than attracting them. So be very careful where you rake. A quick, experimental drag in an area close by is always a good idea.

There are some lakes which have areas where the bottom is

covered with tough pond weed. It is not always wise to clear an area of those weeds, for tench very often have burrows through them and to rake out a large area would perhaps drive them away to an otherwise undisturbed part of the lake. If the water is clear, and it usually is when it grows milfoil and Canadian pond weed, it is better to find the natural clear patches where the weed has not grown at all, or the tench have uprooted it when feeding. If you bait for a period of days over these patches you will find that the clear area grows larger as the tench grub for the food you have put in.

In one lake I have fished the bottom is covered with a tough weed which is criss-crossed with tunnels which the tench have made. The water is crystal-clear and you can see the tench moving through them and popping out every so often before disappearing into another one. I bait with a very light mix and some pieces of pinched flake which mainly settle on top of the weed, then I scatter several handfuls of maggots which mainly filter through into the tunnels. In the very early morning I fish with my float tackle set so that the flake-baited hook lies on top of the weed. I have excellent sport with tench until the sunlight begins to penetrate the water. Then I set the float to fish about a foot deeper, cast in, and inch it back slowly until the float cocks nicely. I know then that the now maggot-baited hook and cocking shot have dropped into the entrance of a burrow. Sport then continues for another couple of hours or so.

Stout tackle is essential when fishing over tough weeds like those mentioned, for as soon as the fish takes you have to bend the rod into him very severely. If you don't, and he manages to dive into one of the burrows, it is almost impossible to pull him out again.

I am sure this is an instance where raking would be detrimental to the fishing rather than an improvement. At the worst it could drive the fish away, and at best it would mean that I could only catch them while the sun was low. If there were no burrows in the swim they would surely move to an area, when the sun rose, where they were still present. If we are thinking in terms of big tench of 5lb or more I think it best to leave a swim as we find it, using tackle and methods to cope with the conditions rather than try to change things to suit ourselves.

202

Tench have a very curious nature and do not scare too easily. After raking a suitable swim it is not at all unusual to begin catching tench within minutes of the last raking, and many times I have been tossing in quite large balls of groundbait only for the float to sink away almost immediately. This is perhaps the reason why boat fishing for tench is so popular, for no matter how skilful and experienced you are at boat fishing there is inevitably some disturbance, even if it is only the lapping of waves on the side of the boat or small waves emanating from the boat when a cast is made. Such disturbance is often enough to scare away fish like big bream and carp. I am sure it is the cat-like curiosity of tench that attracts them to some disturbances rather than frightens them off.

But this does not mean to say you can be careless in your approach; just that you can get away with some things with tench that you could not with other fish. You should always take advantage of any natural cover, move quietly, and generally behave as though any disturbance *will* scare them. It is better to rely on their curiosity keeping them in the swim when noisy accidents happen, rather than testing them with carelessness.

When you have chosen a swim where you know, or at least hope, you can catch tench, it is wise to bait it for a few days before fishing. Obviously, the longer you can pre-bait the swim before fishing the greater your chances are of making a big catch and catching some big fish. But if you have little time to spare, or the water is too far away for you to visit regularly, even one day's pre-baiting will enhance your chances.

If you can manage only one pre-baiting session, then make it a good one. Rake the swim if the bottom is suitable for it and lace the area with mashed bread; scatter in as many lobworms as you can get your hands on, and throw in half a gallon of maggots. That may seem like a lot of free feed, but on a typical tench lake there will not be anything left on the following day when you arrive to fish.

On the morning you fish throw in just a little mashed bread, a few lobs, and a few handfuls of maggots. Then see how it goes, and what bait the tench seem to prefer. Once you know—and let us say the tench want maggots—then you can scatter maggots all over the swim while you are fishing. I like using two rods when tench fishing, with an alternative bait on the other rod. Tench very often go off one bait and onto another very quickly and you can sometimes sit there waiting for a bite, maybe thinking they have gone off feed, when all the time they have 'switched on' to another bait.

Let us assume that the swim, as is usually the case, is a marginal one and perfectly suitable for float fishing. You will need a rod, or rods, of about 12ft long, with an all-through action and a test-curve of 1lb to 1¼lb. The reel will be a fixed-spool and the line 4lb to 6lb b.s., depending on absence or otherwise of snags and size of fish. Let us say you are fishing in the vicinity of lilies and the fish average 4lb. You expect to catch one or two 5-pounders and know there is even a chance of a 6-pounder. So you thread the rod with a 6lb line.

The water is flat-calm, and five feet deep, so you use a small antenna float attached to the line bottom end only. A size 14 spade-end hook is tied to the line which will be suitable for fishing a bunch of three maggots. The second rod is geared up, only this time with a size 8 hook for flake, crust, paste and lobworm fishing, depending on the fish's fancy. The float is set at eighteen inches over-depth and a single BB shot is pinched onto the line fifteen inches from the hook, which is heavy enough with the 2BB locking shot to cock the float. This is a simple, very old laying-on technique which has never been improved for general float fishing on the bottom. It is simplicity itself, and simplicity is very efficient.

You have thrown a few samples of hookbait—groundbait, lobworms and maggots—into the swim as soon as you arrived. It is still quite dark and you have tackled up well away from the water with the aid of a slim pen-torch which you have held in your mouth to leave both hands free for threading line and tying knots. By the time you have assembled the landing net and propped it against the rushes within easy reach of your left hand; set up the rod-rests; positioned the chair and laid your baitboxes and tackle box around you, it is breaking daylight. The grass is wet with dew, moorhens and coots are beginning to scamper across the water and a fine mist shrouds the surface. It is a typical, exciting tench morning.

When the floats are cast, the one in the middle of the swim

above a bunch of maggots and the one on the left of the swim above a big lobworm, you can only vaguely make out the orange tips in the half light and through the swirling mist. It is not quite light enough yet to see if any bubbles are popping on the surface.

Twenty minutes pass without even a tremble on one of the floats. It is light enough now to see the surface around the floats but there is no sign of feeding fish. But to the right, about ten yards away, a big dorsal and black back silently humps the surface. A tench, no mistaking it. It should not be long now.

Five minutes later the water is still and bubbleless, but you see the maggot-holding float tilt ever so slightly to and fro, like a schoolteacher wagging his finger at a naughty pupil. You watch it so intently you are taken by surprise when you glance at the lob-holding float and find it has disappeared! A lift of the rod and a sharp tug to sink in the size 8 hook and you feel the jab-jabbing of a tench when it first feels the hook. The jabbing turns into a surging run which you clamp down on before he gets too confident. You bring him towards the net quite easily, but before you can get smug about it he goes off on another long run and the line slices through the stems of a couple of the thinly-scattered lily pads. You bring him back and after another short jab-jabbing session you slide him into the net. At around 4lb he is smaller than average for this water but a nice promise of what is yet to come. You slide the hook out of his top lip with your curved artery forceps and slide him back into the water.

You retrieve the maggot rod, which has shown no more promise since the float tilted a few minutes ago, and prop it in the rushes for the time being. If the tench want lobworm that is what you will give them. There is no point in fishing with two rods if one is going to prove a nuisance every time you hook a fish. The second rod will come in handy for experimenting with when the tench show signs of going off feed, or at least going off lobworms.

Another fat lob is nicked onto the hook and re-cast into the swim, and as the float settles you are delighted to see that now there are several patches of bubbles popping at the surface. Before you can rest the rod the float slides across the surface and then disappears quite determinedly. A quick flick of the wrist and the fish is on, 5½lb this time: a good fish.

You catch three more tench on lobs in the next thirty minutes, but for fifteen minutes following you fail to get another decent bite. The bubble patches are still evident and the float flickers occasionally, but giving nothing at which to strike. So you retrieve the tackle and swap the lobworm for a pinch of flake. All to no purpose, for you are still waiting for a bite twenty minutes later.

You take up your second rod, bait it with a bunch of three maggots, and cast a yard from the first rod. Still nothing, not even a flicker from either float now, but bubbles are still popping at the surface in haphazard patches over the baited area.

Your retrieve the bread rod and revert to lob, only this time with a two-inch lob-tail. Two minutes after re-casting you are into another tench that eventually turns the scales at 6lb 5oz; your biggest of the morning so far.

For the next hour or so you take a few more tench, the last three falling to a bunch of maggots. But since the sun has risen higher in the sky and the light has been able to penetrate the water, the bites have become extremely tentative, and many times you have retrieved the tackle only to find that the maggots were stretched and you have seen no indication of interference on the float whatsoever.

The 'lift' method is called for. You have reached the stage where the tench are merely mouthing the bait without moving off with it, and ordinary laying-on tactics are not sensitive enough to register bites. The principle of the lift method is very simple, yet extremely effective. The float and weight are arranged in such a way that as soon as the shot is moved the float's antenna rises in the water and could eventually keel over to lie flat on the surface.

The single BB shot is slid down the line to one to two inches from the hook. You then place the rod in two rod-rests and draw the float towards you until the tight line pulls the bottom of the float down and the sight-bob sits at the surface. You can see then, that as soon as the shot is dislodged, and its influence on the float is cancelled out, the float will slowly rise until all of the antenna is revealed.

Small baits are the ideal partners for the lift method, for when

206

tench are in the mood to necessitate lift-method fishing they are also in the mood to take small baits.

Occasionally, you need to strike as soon as the float begins to rise, but more often than not it is best to wait until it is fully risen. You should, however, take each situation as it comes, and strike according to the demands on that particular day. You cast, place the rod in the two rod-rests, and then turn the reel handle until only the sight-bob remains visible.

The tiny bubbles are still evident. Even more so in fact, and you guess that the tench are rooting in earnest for the maggots that lie among the bottom mud. To keep them interested you scatter a handful of maggots around the float.

Only moments later, the float dithers, then slowly rises in the water. You grab the rod and strike all in one motion, but there is no resistance: you missed it. You examine the maggots and find them still wriggly and very much alive, so you cast to the same spot again, rest the rod, and set the float once more.

The next bite comes almost immediately: a dither, then a lift, and you resist the temptation to strike. The float seems to stop rising and then suddenly falls over on the surface. This time your strike is rewarded with a bent rod and minutes later a stocky tench of near on 6lb is being slipped into your keepnet.

So much for a description of a typical, classical tenching session, and it is perhaps fortunate that most tench fishing follows a similar pattern. There are situations, however, that demand an entirely different approach. This is long-range tench fishing, made necessary for various reasons. One reason is that a water may not have suitable margins to attract tench, another is that the water may be so popular the tench have become margin-shy and prefer to spend the majority of their time in comparative safety.

The approach in such a situation should follow almost the same lines as the one used for big bream at long-range, which include the methods used for groundbaiting and the recommended tackle set-ups. Obviously though, the line should be stepped up from 4lb to 5lb or 6lb. At long range, however, you will probably be able to get away with 5lb b.s. even with the biggest of tench, for great distances elasticates the fight to a degree and gives you an extra safety margin.

In gravel and sand pits, and other hard-bottomed waters, the swimfeeder can be deadly for tench at long range. A block-end 'feeder (the Peter Drennan 'Feederlink' being about the best) can be filled with maggots and used with almost the same efficiency as 'feeders on a river.

The most important factor is accurate casting, no less so in stillwaters as it is in rivers. There is little point in leaving a heap of maggots here, there and everywhere, which may tend to split the tench into several groups. Pinpoint accuracy is not necesssary, of course, but casting within, say, a four-yard circle should be regarded as maximum 'spread'.

I usually stop the 'feeder about two feet from the hook, and a few minutes after casting I reel in two feet of line. This means I have drawn the baited hook into the thick of the escaping maggots. Regular filling and casting of the 'feeder is not so essential as it is on rivers, for you have no current to carry away the feed. How often you replenish the 'feeder's contents is according to how well, or otherwise, the fish are responding.

There are some waters that hold very few tench, but usually they are exceptionally big fish that warrant attention. I have often found that these big fellows rarely wander far from dense weedbeds, as though their lack of numbers somehow undermines their safety. Or it may simply mean that because there are so few of them they do not need to search for food, but can find everything they need in the confines of their weedy havens. I am more inclined to go along with the latter theory.

Natural baits such as swan mussels come into their own where these big, almost solitary fish are concerned. Clearing a gap in the weed and pre-baiting will more likely have a detrimental effect rather than the usual attracting one. So the swim should be left as natural as possible, and tackle used to combat the conditions.A good idea is to collect a dozen or so mussels for bait and use some of the biggest ones for free feed. You simply smash them up, shells and all, in a bucket, and scatter them over the swim.

To pull big tench from thick weed an 8lb line is not too heavy. The hook needs to be strong too, and since we are going to use a big piece of mussel, maybe even a whole one, a size 4 should be about right.

I like to use a whole mussel as bait, one about the size of a matchbox. After disposing of the shell I push the hook right through the hard, orange pad and then stick it in again lower down in the fleshy part. The hook point should be masked so that it does not snag so readily in the weed, but should only be masked behind a soft, fleshy part of the mussel so as not to impede the penetration of the hook when you have to strike.

The tackle is a simple free-line rig. Just the line and hook and nothing else. A standard carp rod of 1½lb test-curve and a fixed-spool reel completes the set-up.

The technique is to cast the mussel on top of the weed, then drag it off and let it sink. No indicator is necessary, for you should hold the rod all the time, with just a loop of line hanging from between butt-ring and reel, which can be held lightly between finger and thumb. Every two or three minutes you should wind this loop of line onto the spool and then twitch the mussel through the weed until you have a similar loop of line between finger and thumb.

Holding the line is not to facilitate touch-legering, for bites on mussel are usually bold and the tench will whip the line quite easily from your light grip. Holding the line, however, makes it easier on your concentration, allowing you to glance up occasionally to give your eyes a rest.

Frequent snagging will inevitably occur, despite your masking the hook point. It should be treated, however, as a natural hazard of the technique, for there is very little you can do about it. Anyway, the weed will usually break before the 8lb line does.

The spool clutch should be screwed hard down, for when a fish is hooked you must bend into it in no uncertain terms, and keep pulling very severely until the fish is forced out of the weed. If you should once let him get his head round then all is lost. Immediate, aggressive tactics are the only way, for you are relying on hauling the tench straight out of the weed even before he can think, let alone react. Finesse has no part in this kind of fishing, so if you prefer to have a sophisticated fight from a fish, then forget about weedbed fishing. The weed will beat you every time.

Contrary to the brutal, heavyweight tactics of weedbed

fishing, there are many times when you need to scale down to delicate, featherweight methods to catch tench. These are the times when tench become preoccupied with minute food items to the exclusion of all else. It is mainly natural food creatures, such as bloodworms, with which they become obsessed, but very often we bring about this preoccupation with our own baits; maggots in particular.

It is a conditioning factor; they become so used to picking up single maggots their minds refuse to accept anything other than a single maggot as food. It is preoccupation at its worst, when the only way of catching them is, obviously, to use a single maggot. That is, if you are fishing in open water and do not need to put unnecessary pressure on the small hook you are obliged to use with such a tiny bait.

Sometimes, the preoccupation is not quite so acute, and they will accept two maggots, or even three. A strong, size 16 hook— a Drennan 'Super Specialist' is one of the best available— should be selected, with as fine a line as one dare use in the conditions prevailing. These items, coupled with a very delicate 'lift' rig, will get you the bites.

The real problem begins when you hook a big tench, especially if there are weeds nearby, which is highly likely where tench are concerned. The best playing technique in this situation is to 'nurse' them. Do not apply any pressure whatsoever, apart from keeping the line reasonably taut so as to maintain a hookhold. You will find that the tench will not usually bore off with the same aggression as when you are able to give him some stick with sensible tackle.

It will, however, take you a very long time to land each fish, for you need to rely so much on luck. You need luck and not a small amount of skill to steer him towards the landing net without upsetting him too much. Apply just that little bit too much pressure and he will raise his hackles and head full-steam for the nearest snag—and on delicate tackle there will be sweet nothing you can do about it!

You must bear in mind that you are not going to catch a lot of tench on such fine tackle, for although bites are no problem, you will spend most of the time simply hanging on to the rod while the fish continues to amble around the swim until he is too

Graham Marsden and a 5lb 10oz tench he took using the 'lift-method'.

tired to offer much more of a fight. While this is going on it is not certain that any tench who are in the swim at that time are going to stay there.

Another thing which you should remember is that it is so easy to fall into the trap of thinking that fine tackle is demanded when it really is not. Always try a variety of baits, and anything else which may do the trick while still using appropriate tackle, before you resort to delicate gear.

Light tackle for any big fish should only be used as a last resort. There is no merit in hooking fish that break you. Anglers who use fine tackle all the time are more preoccupied, or brainwashed, than the fish they are trying to catch.

Index

HNV baits 84–5

Jones, Richard, 167
judging results, xv

keepnet, 7
kiting, 41, 65

landing net, 7
lateral line, 47
leader, braided, 134
leader, bream, 45–7
lift-method, 113–14, 206–7
lilies, 200
lines, 6
    barbel, 36
    bream, 59
    carp, 81
    chub, 98, 100
    crucian, 111
    dace, 121–3
    eel, 133
    perch, 146
    pike, 160
    roach, 175
    rudd, 185
    tench, 204, 207–9
link-leger, 11, 60, 125
link-swivel, 134
lobworms, hooking, 147
location, 53–5
Loch Lomond, 153

Macclesfield Canal, 168, 174
Middleton, Len, 87
    milfoil, 202
multiple particle baits, 85–6
multiplier reel, 160

National Anguilla Club, 129
night fishing, 16–20
    checking surroundings, 18–19
    good company, 19–21
    lights, 17
    noting times, 19
    what to wear, 17
Norfolk Broads, 153

Optonic bite alarm, 9, 134
Oxford T.C. Pit, 52

paternoster, 11, 60, 142, 190
    running, 10, 146
patience, xv
peacock quill, 141–2, 186
pendulum cast, 182
Penney, William, 167
perch, 136–49
    availability of, 136

effect of light, 149
hot-spot, 145
hunt by sight, 139
locating, 144
record, 138
runs, 148
summer, 140–4
swim-bladder, 148
winter, 144–9
pike, 150–66
    camouflage, 151
    clock pattern, 154
    dead-baiting, 156–60
    feeding times, 162
    float, 163
    float paternoster, 163–4
    growth rate, 152–3
    hot-spots, 163
    lateral line, 152
    live-baiting, 155–6
    location, 154, 162–3
    location—river, 164–5
    lure fishing, 153–5
    period of fast, 162
    record, 151
    'shoal bait', 159
    speed and power, 152
    tackle, 160–1
    techniques, 163–4
    teeth, 151–2
    trotting, 165
    weather, 163
    where found, 152
planning and preparing, 2
playing fish
    handling, 133
    pumping, 133
pre-baiting, xi–xii
    frequency of, 56–7
predators
    bream, 72–3
    eels, 130
    perch, 137
    pike, 151–2
preoccupation, 26
priming, or rolling, 48–50, 184
punt fishing 21–3

Queenford Lagoon, 52
quiver-tip, 126

radar system, 41, 47
record fish, 24–5
Redmire Pool, 75
reels, 6
roach, 167–82
    effect of light, 180
    effect of wind, 179–80

215